Little *Alf*

Enjoy! He's a
funny ing —
Love 2019 —
Gramma &
Pappy &
Loie

Little Alf

Hannah Russell

with Jordan Paramor

sphere

SPHERE

First published in Great Britain in 2017 by Sphere

5 7 9 10 8 6

A CIP catalogue record for this book
is available from the British Library.

ISBN 978-0-7515-6891-2

Typeset in Garamond by M Rules
Printed and bound in Great Britain by Clays Ltd, Elcograf S.p.A.

Papers used by Sphere are from well-managed forests
and other responsible sources.

Sphere
An imprint of
Little, Brown Book Group
Carmelite House
50 Victoria Embankment
London EC4Y 0DZ

An Hachette UK Company
www.hachette.co.uk

www.littlebrown.co.uk

*To Alfie, you make my
world complete*

Contents

Prologue

This is the story of how a very small pony with a very big personality came into my life and turned it upside down in the best possible way. You see, my Shetland pony, Little Alf, was born with dwarfism, meaning he's only a teeny twenty-eight inches tall (to put that in perspective, he's the same height as a greyhound!).

But what he lacks in height he makes up for in determination and charm.

From meeting royalty to getting royally told off, the last three years with Alf have been one long, wonderful adventure, and I'm sure there are many more amazing times to come.

Life for ponies that aren't considered 'perfect' can be unpredictable, and they don't always have a happy ending, so people often say to me they think I saved Little Alf. But he came into my life just when I needed him the most, so really, I think we kind of saved each other . . .

From the moment Alf and I met there was a connection. I can't really explain it but it was like we were *supposed* to be together. I may have changed his life when I took him in, but he changed mine right back.

When I first saw Alf he was a fluffy, forlorn, lost little thing. His mum had rejected him, he was surplus to his breeder's requirements, and his future didn't look good. He was standing in a field on his own with his tiny legs submerged in mud and he looked so sad and lonely.

I wanted to dash over, pick him up and run away with him as fast as my legs would carry me (which, let's face it, would have been *a lot* faster than his legs could carry him). When I look back now, I can't believe that was the same funny, feisty, attitude-packed pony so many people have come to know and love. Alf truly is a one-off.

Prologue

Whether it's starting the day with a cup of tea together, or the moment he steals the marshmallows off the top of my hot chocolate each evening, every moment with Alf is magical. Even the really, really embarrassing ones, of which there have been many.

I can't wait to tell you all about him; from that first meeting, to his glamorous life as a model, award winner and social media star. It's only a matter of time before Hollywood comes calling . . .

Chapter 1

And We're Off!

Before we get to the very important bit when we meet Little Alf, I'm going to give you a bit of background about me and my love of animals. And, in particular, my love of rescuing creatures that need a bit of extra love and care.

I was born in Scarborough on 18 January 1997 and my family and I lived there until I was four. Even back then I was fascinated by horses and my first ever experience of these amazing beasts was also one of my earliest memories – riding donkeys on Scarborough beach when I was three years old. My parents have a photo of me sitting on the back of a donkey with a massive smile on my face. Some young kids are afraid of big animals like that but I absolutely loved them. I was always hassling my parents to let me go and 'sit on the funny donkey'.

I've had pets since I was small and I can't imagine what my life would have been like without them. I've always felt a real connection with animals (the only thing I'm not keen on are slugs) and I feel calm and relaxed when I'm around them.

Our first family pet was a German Shepherd called Misty, who my parents got a year before I was born. Apparently as soon as I learnt to walk, I followed her everywhere. She was such a lovely, friendly girl and I always felt protected when she was around.

Mum and dad rescued Misty when she was two because she'd been used for breeding and the breeders no longer wanted her, so she needed a good home. My granddad was a policeman and he worked with German Shepherds all the time, and when he told my mum and dad about her they said they'd give her a home.

Tragically Misty had recently lost a whole litter of

puppies and she kept having phantom pregnancies, so our vet said it would be a good idea for her to have one more litter. When I was two she had six puppies, but sadly three of those died. My granddad took one of the puppies, the owner of the puppies' father had another, and the final one, who we called Hickson, stayed with us.

Hickson was born with a cleft palate and no eyelids. He also had a bad skin condition and because of all his ailments my parents knew it would difficult to find someone who wanted to take him on. Sadly, people want perfect puppies, and even I'll admit that Hickson came with a lot challenges.

Because he didn't have eyelids the only way you could tell he was asleep was by his snoring – his eyes would still be wide open! He also couldn't blink, meaning his eyes watered constantly so my parents were always wiping them with special tissues and making sure they didn't get infected. His cleft palate meant that the front of his mouth was split in two, so when he ate food would get caught in the gap. We used to have to pat him on the back to dislodge it. I know that sounds a bit gross but he was such a sweet dog we really didn't mind.

When the puppies were tiny and people came to

see them they'd coo over the others and then they'd point at Hickson and say things like, 'What's wrong with that one? He looks weird.' But from day one he was my favourite.

But being different definitely didn't affect Hickson's personality. I don't think he had a clue he wasn't the same as his siblings and he was really happy and confident. He was black and brown like a normal German Shepherd but he was also very fluffy. When I was young I thought he was quite wolf-like, but he was the softest, most affectionate boy ever.

Hickson and I became best friends and we did everything together – my mum says that we were completely inseparable. I used to roll around on the floor with him and we'd cuddle up in his bed – he was one hundred per cent my dog. When we both got a bit older he'd sit on the front of my skateboard and we'd whizz around our patio. We did that his entire life, right up until the day he died.

When Hickson was young we were told by a vet that he would probably only live until he was three because of all of his health issues, but thankfully he lived until he was ten and he was always full of energy and so happy. I guess Hickson was the first animal I rescued. He had such a great life with us.

My mum would often joke that we were like each other's shadows and she's totally right. I still miss him now.

I was really close to my family growing up and I count myself lucky because even though my brother, John, and I are very different – he's a bit more shy (and doesn't talk as much!) – we have always got on well. He's only a year older than me and we're good friends – we hang out with each other out of choice, not familial ties! I know some of my friends who have brothers or sisters that drive them mad. We never really argued and when he's away at university, where he's studying computing, I find myself missing him.

I think some of our family's closeness has to do with the fact that when I was four, my mum started to become really ill. She was tired all the time, her body ached and she was having these horrendous headaches, but despite going to see several doctors she couldn't get a diagnosis. It was such a frustrating time for her. She went downhill quickly, to the point where she was finding it hard to get out of bed each morning.

The doctors kept insisting she had depression and tried to put her on anti-depressants, but Mum knew that wasn't the cause. Eventually she insisted on being referred to the hospital for some tests and it was then that they discovered she was suffering from ME, also known as Chronic Fatigue Syndrome.

As a result of this, my parents decided to move to the Yorkshire Dales, where my mum was brought up, so she could be closer to her parents. It meant they could help out with my brother and me when Mum was going through a bad patch. Dad owns his own business so he was working really hard, and there were days when Mum found it hard to put one foot in front of the other, let alone take care of two young kids.

I helped out as much as I could, especially when I knew Mum was having a bad day. I used to stand on a chair to wash the dishes, and would count out her change for her when we went to the shops. I'm sure that's why I was so good at maths at school! My family say I had to grow up really quickly so I could be there for my mum, but I didn't know any different. Dad reckons I didn't play out with my friends as much as some children because I didn't like leaving Mum, but I really didn't mind. My Mum is incredible and even now, she's my best friend. We can talk about anything and I laugh with her more than I do with anyone.

Mum had ME for around ten years in total and then slowly but surely she started to get better. It's hard because doctors still don't really know how to cure ME, so really it's a case of finding out ways to treat it yourself. Mum did a lot of self-healing – she tried reiki and aromatherapy and all sorts. She also made sure she ate well and took lots of vitamins, as well as educating herself on the best ways to overcome illness. Mum still has her off days where she feels tired and run down, but she's so much better than she was. She's even started her own painting business and she's more active than she's ever been.

While this was all going on my obsession with horses continued to grow as I got older and I used to watch every horse programme that was on TV – all my favourite things revolved around horses. I read all of Linda Chapman's *My Secret Unicorn* books and when I was seven I started writing letters to her – I've still got about fifty to sixty postcards she sent to me over the years! I remember getting my first one and feeling like I had heard from a superstar. It made me feel so special. I still speak to Linda every now and again over Facebook and she's so nice.

I don't know where my fixation came from as no

one else in my immediate family was horsey. My parents didn't ride and John was much more interested in computer games than anything else, so I was the only one who was horse mad. I don't know if it had anything to do with growing up surrounded by farmland and seeing horses every day of my life, but I loved them above everything else, and still do!

After my early donkey rides, the first time I rode a real pony was when I was five. I started going to the Bainbridge Riding Centre and having regular lessons. I mainly rode a lovely horse called Timmy. He had arthritis so he was a bit of a plodder but I didn't mind. He was a type of pony called a Welsh Section C, so he was really dinky. I rode him every Saturday and he was amazing with me.

I absolutely loved it there, but still I dreamed of owning my very own horse, and one day, completely unexpectedly, that dream came true.

I was six years old when my mum told me about a fourteen-year-old Cob called Badger. Tragically his owner had died from cancer and Badger went through a terrible grieving period. He became very depressed as there was no one around to give him the love and attention he needed and as a result his health went rapidly downhill. When my mum's cousin Carine, who had been friends with his owner, realised this, she stepped in and said she'd take care of him. She owns a large working farm so had the space for him, but she knew that with all her other animals to look after it would be impossible to keep him long-term.

By the time Carine went to pick him up Badger was very overweight. Everyone was shocked by how quickly he'd gone from being a happy, healthy horse to a shadow of his former self.

He'd gone from being incredibly well looked after and ridden every day to not being ridden at all. He was left in a field on his own and the lack of exercise and the fact he was depressed meant that the weight had kept piling on.

Carine had begun to nurse Badger back to health when, one day out of the blue, she asked my parents if I'd like him. They knew I'd be absolutely over the moon, and thankfully they said yes. I think my mum and dad were a bit worried about how much work it would involve but they knew I'd help with the mucking out and feeding as much as I could.

When I first saw Badger I ran straight up to him and gave him a hug. Well, sort of. He was about twice the size of me and very 'curvy' so it was a bit tricky.

Believe it or not, although he'd already lost weight while he was living with Carine, he lost another nine stone after he came to live with us.

We were living in a house in Harmby at the time and it didn't have stables, so we kept Badger in a large field at the back. My parents would look after him when I was at school, and then I'd chip in whenever I was around.

Even though he wasn't in the best shape I thought Badger was perfect because he was mine. It didn't even cross my mind that he was a bit rough around the edges. He was such a handsome boy. Typically Cobs are small with short legs and a heavy build, so he was never going to have the slender physique of a racehorse.

He wasn't the happiest horse in the world at first, but that soon started to change and after a few weeks of being with us he began to get his spirit back. It was amazing because I was able to actually watch it happening, and it was such a brilliant transformation. The more weight he lost the more energy he had. I even started riding him, but my parents and I still felt like something wasn't right.

I had a lovely bond with him, but I could tell by the way he was reacting to me when I was riding him that everything wasn't as it should be. He was bucking all the time, and that often happens when a horse is injured in some way.

And that's when we discovered he had a dislocated neck.

It's not a common thing to happen, and when it does owners often don't realise. Because the horse is in pain it starts being naughty and playing up. That makes the owner think they need to be ever stricter with them and they'll begin to discipline them, which can make things even worse.

It was impossible to know that his neck was out of place just from looking at him, but we got him checked out by a vet to try and determine why he was so nervous.

The vet spotted the problem straight away, which was such a relief. He did some physio on Badger and then he snapped his neck back into place. It was such an awful sound. It kind of echoed, and even though I was so young I can still remember it clearly. Badger's neck still clicks to this day as a result of that injury, and because he's a bit arthritic now sometimes you can really hear it, but it doesn't seem to bother him at all.

Following his treatment, bit by bit Badger started

to hold his head higher, and he started to recognise us and get excited when we went to see him. The horse world was new to my family but Carine and some of the other horse owners at the stables gave us tips on how to look after him. Everything else we had to learn as we went along by reading books and websites.

Once I had Badger I became more horse mad than ever. I upped my horse riding lessons to three times a week and on Saturdays I'd go to classes where I'd learn how to care for and groom horses. My whole life revolved around Badger and learning how to look after him. I even kept a diary where I wrote down everything we got up to. It could be the smallest thing, like going for a walk around the paddock, but I loved him so much I wanted to remember every little detail.

I actually kept diaries from the age of six to sixteen. I read through some of them recently and they're so funny. Anyone else would find them really boring but I'm so happy I've got a record of all the things Badger and I did in those early days. I even wrote a story about Badger, so maybe that got me in training for my later writing . . .

These are a few extracts from my early diaries:

25 July 2008

I went riding today it was sooo much fun and so hot. It was twenty-five degrees so we only took it steady, as I didn't want Badger getting too hot. Next week I am going on holiday to Portugal but I can't bear the thought of leaving Badger and Pepper. I really don't want to go. He's being looked after by a friend so I'm sure he will be fine. I feel so sad about leaving them.

24 August 2008

Yesterday I did my first ever show with Badger. I was so nervous, but he kept me happy. I did a clear round jumping and even got a rosette which is now pinned up on the fridge in the kitchen!!!! I also did a dressage class, but the judge didn't like the fact I had the wrong colour gloves on. Mum told me not to worry, she said we still looked nice! I'm so proud of Badger. He is my little star.

11 October 2008

Today was my first day at my new pony club!! I had the best time. It's not a real pony club, it's one we have made up with friends. I went there with Badger and met my friends, and some new friends too! We tacked up, then mounted and warmed up the horses in the ménage and then we did some jumping which was sooo good. I don't have very good balance but I will get better with time. Then we had dinner and went out for a trek around the fields and I GALLOPED for the first time!! It was so much fun. We got back at three p.m. and then went home. It was the best day ever! Badger is now really tired and so am I!

23 May 2009

I've not written in my diary for a couple of months since I've been on the mend. I had a few bad falls with Badger as he keeps bucking. But we weren't sure why. Lots of people thought Badger was being naughty but Mum and I knew there was something wrong. I don't think Badger would ever want to hurt me really.

Mum decided to get a back specialist for horses to come to see Badger and guess what? He was in so much pain his neck was dislocated and his body was really sore. No wonder he kept bucking, he was trying to tell me something. I feel so guilty for riding him when he was in pain and can't understand why nobody knew. Now he's on the mend and is on the way to recovery. I'm not allowed to ride Badger for four weeks but I don't care. I just don't want him to be poorly.

27 November 2009

A new friend.

We have a new friend for Badger and Pepper. His name is Patch, but we have renamed him Paddy because we want him to have a fresh start with us. Paddy is a year old and he's been a bit neglected. He's very shy and nervous. He has stitches on his nose and hair missing and hoof-marks all over his body. He's really skinny. We've only had him a day but he seems to be happier than yesterday. I think he knows he's safe now . . . Badger seems to like him – he keeps kissing his nose.

The next horse I got was Pepper. My parents and I really wanted a companion for Badger because we were worried he was lonely, so when we heard about a horse that needed re-homing he sounded perfect.

Pepper had really bad sweet itch, which is an allergic reaction to midges, and because he lived next to a wood to he kept getting attacked by them. Where we were keeping Badger there weren't many midges so it would suit Pepper much better.

He was in a terrible state when we first got him. His coat was falling out and he'd itch constantly. He was always biting and scratching his skin and because of that he'd get blisters. His fur would come out in clumps. He was so uncomfortable, bless him. We were so worried about him, but after some treatment from the vet it started to clear up.

I didn't ever ride him because he's a miniature Shetland so he's far too small, but he was the perfect field mate for Badger.

I'm not joking, it was like Badger instantly became Pepper's dad. When they first met they accepted each other straight away. I wonder if Badger could sense that Pepper had been through a difficult time himself. If you met a person who had come from a difficult background you would probably react in the same way, and it was almost like Badger had this empathy and understanding for Pepper.

Badger went for a walk around the field and Pepper followed him like it was the most natural thing in the world. They were grooming each other and playing. Pepper didn't know how to eat food from a bucket, or how to be around people, and daddy Badger stepped in and showed him the way.

They soon became best friends and they're still inseparable now. Pepper is such a sweet boy, he's really soft and tame and affectionate, and Badger always looks out for him.

When I was about ten I started going to pony club every Saturday, and shortly afterwards I began competing in various competitions. Compared to some pony clubs mine wasn't that strict because really it was just me and some of my friends getting together to have a nice time.

I didn't do the circuit like a lot of kids do. The 'circuit' is basically where you go to different venues, like country houses or really posh arenas. It's very strict and you have to have the right equipment and clothing and say the right things. Not being on the circuit suited me much better because I didn't feel comfortable when I had to be on my best behaviour.

I did try out a few other pony clubs but a lot of them were very snobby, which didn't suit me at all. The girls on the circuit took it all so seriously and they were very competitive, but I wanted to enjoy my horse, not use him to show off. No one seemed very friendly with each other at the serious events, but my group all mucked in and had fun together. The other girls were quite catty too, and I was never into the whole 'talking about people behind their back' thing. A lot of them had known each other for years and they all went to the same expensive schools. I didn't fit in, which was fine with me.

My pony camp was very down to earth and you could rock up wearing what you wanted and no one would judge you, whereas at others you had to look perfect – what they wore was almost like a uniform. You had to have a different outfit for each discipline, like dressage and cross country, whereas my mates and I tipped up in a hoodie and jodhpurs.

My friends and I did the same things that other camps did, but we had a real laugh. We were simply there for the love of horses, we weren't thinking about winning the Olympics. Far from it. As well as doing cross country and show jumping we used to play games like football with the horses. One day we played a game where we all put plastic cups on our head filled with Skittles. The aim was to keep the Skittles in the pot while we were riding around the ménage. I'm pretty sure they're not going to be introducing that into the Olympics anytime soon.

A ménage is like a big sandy play area with a fence around it. It's a paddock with sand, basically. I always think of it a little beach, but I don't think proper horsey types would approve of me saying that. I think you'd be in a bit of trouble if you suddenly lay down to do a bit of sunbathing.

You often do jumps in a ménage, and there are mirrors up so you can watch yourself as you ride and see what you need to improve on. You basically do a lot of practising in them, and people will use them to perfect their techniques if they're gearing up for shows. Or, if you're me, you use them to have fun with your horses and learn tricks!

Cobs can be quite athletic but they're better known for doing cross-country jumps. Badger was very small compared to my friends' ponies because they were all racehorse size so I knew he would never be able to do proper high-level stuff, but I didn't mind. To me he was perfect. I think a lot of people would have traded Badger in as they got more advanced and became a better rider. After a few years, people did often say to me it was time I got a new horse, but I didn't want to. I loved Badger so much, even though I kept falling off him all the time.

The thing is, Badger wasn't terribly well behaved and he was easily startled, so most Saturdays I'd end up on the floor at least once. The combination of his unpredictability and my dubious balance meant that I'd often find myself rolling around in mud while Badger gazed off into the distance, oblivious to the fact that I may have hurt myself. Thankfully I didn't ever break any bones or anything. I'd end up a bit bruised and battered but there was no lasting damage. Or so I thought . . .

In the end, though, I stopped being embarrassed about my numerous falls. It happened so often it became a bit of a running joke with my mates, and sometimes they'd take bets on how long it would be until I was flat on my back, laughing even though I was filthy and in pain.

However, though Badger may not have been the most skilled horse you'd ever meet, I was still determined to win competitions with him. He may have been disruptive but I wasn't going to give up on him that easily. There were times when we'd be in the middle of competing and I'd topple off and Badger would storm out, but I always shrugged it off. Everyone would look on in horror and that was usually when people would say I needed to get a new horse, but I knew Badger had it in him. As I saw it, I had no option but to go out and do my best, and if people laughed at us, which they did, so what? Badger and I held our heads up high and we were proud of every little achievement we had.

The horse world can be pretty awful. It's so snobby and it's cliquey. If you don't have the fastest horse or the right name people don't want to know you. And on top of that you have to have the top-branded products or people look down on you. It's not a happy, inclusive kind of world. People end up feeling left out if their pony isn't quite up to standard. The industry and the people in it can be so bitchy and it's so unnecessary. Some of us just enjoy horse riding, we're not doing it to try and show off our wealth.

Katie Price comes up against a huge amount of this but at least she has tried to change things. I've always loved everything she's done with her horses.

People in the horse world don't like her because she doesn't fit the stereotype, but I admire her for that. The stereotype of a horse competition is that everyone wears the same thing and they end up looking like they're in a girl band, whereas Katie will turn up in bright colours looking fun and without a care for what anyone thinks. At the end of the day, the brands you wear don't make you a better or worse rider.

I must admit, I've always been much more of a Katie Price than someone who fits that stereotype. Other people would turn up at competitions in their crisp white shirts and black jodhpurs and I'd be in a neon pink top and a purple hat. I was lucky that I was allowed to compete at all because sometimes you get disqualified if you're not in the right clothes.

Sometimes I'd enter shows and I wasn't even properly acknowledged because it was pretty obvious that I wasn't going to win anything with poor Badger. I think that was so rude. I mean, it would have been fair enough if I'd taken Pepper along to a show-jumping competition because that would have been utterly ridiculous (and hilarious!), but Badger had just as much chance as any other pony.

Badger and I did eventually win a competition

when I was fourteen. It was a mini show-jumping competition and it was a nice feeling, but I still didn't think it was the most important thing in the world. Badger got extra pony nuts that night and I got to pin my first ever rosette on his stable door, but it wasn't exactly a life-changing event! We won quite a few more rosettes after that, which usually went on a pinboard on my bedroom wall. I won a couple later with Paddy, my other horse, too. They were real achievements, but I think it's fair to say I was never what you'd call Royal Ascot material.

Despite us not setting the competition world alight, I wouldn't have changed anything about my horses. It shocks me the way horses are treated sometimes. They're such incredible creatures, and all such individual characters, but certain people have little respect for them and will simply dispose of them when they no longer meet their needs. This will only change if people with influence are willing to do something, and I can't see anyone in a position of power being brave enough to go against the grain and stand up and say things are wrong. For instance, I hate the hunting world. I know chasing foxes is banned now but people still do it and it's horrific. It's so outdated and cruel. The dogs are bred to be

hunters, and once they become surplus to requirements they're often put down. So many animals suffer
for what is just a cruel sport.

I'd had Badger and Pepper for six years when I
heard about another horse that needed a good home,
a lovely boy called Paddy. We saw him for sale online
and he was in such a state we wanted to buy him
immediately so we could get him away from whatever
horrible situation he was in. The previous owners
advertised him as being five years old and ready to
be ridden, but we could tell by his photo that wasn't
the case, he looked so much younger.

My parents and I went to see him and we had to
drive down this weird lane in the middle of a housing
estate. We came to this really boggy field that was
surrounded by barbed wire and saw this poor horse
that can have only been about a year old. The guy
selling him asked if I wanted to ride him and we were
disgusted. No horse should have a saddle on their
back at that age because their bodies are still growing
and developing and you can cause lifelong damage.
Most aren't ready to be ridden regularly until they're
around four or five, and sometimes even older. The
only horses that are ridden when they're younger are
racehorses. They're often ridden from the age of one

or two, and the poor things are retired by the time they're six or seven.

We felt really resentful about handing over money to someone who would treat animals so appallingly, but equally we didn't want to leave Paddy where he was. He looked so unhappy and, really, we'd already made up our minds to take him home.

In the trailer on the way back to Yorkshire poor Paddy kept falling asleep – clearly he was exhausted. It was like he'd breathed a sigh of relief that he was finally out of that awful place. There had been some other horses in the field with him and I felt so bad that we couldn't take them all home with us. I prayed that someone would go and rescue them.

We don't really know exactly what had happened to Paddy while he was in that field but when we got him home and looked him over we realised he had loads of burn marks and belt scars all over him, and stitches on his nose. He was scared of everything. Though we don't know if he was actually set on fire, he was certainly burned in some way. He was very conscious of his scars and I wish I knew his full history because that might make it easier to understand his erratic behaviour, even now, years later.

You can't see his scars now because his hair has

grown over them but you can definitely tell that what happened affects him to this day. We had to take baby steps and allow him to settle in really slowly so he didn't freak out. He was scared of us, and he'd panic if we started walking towards him. We used to sit on buckets in his field and wait for him to approach us when he was ready so we could build up his trust. We had to stay very still or he'd get freaked out, and we could be there for hours sometimes. But very slowly he started to respond positively, and he began to realise that we weren't going to hurt him. He obviously had a lot of bad memories of his former life and they were hard to shake.

When Paddy started to let us approach him, the next stage was to give him a treat and then walk off so we didn't crowd him. That way he had a positive affirmation and he'd know we were walking over because we were going to do something nice. We'd also put a ball down in the field and walk off, and then we'd go back and pick it up so there was no pressure for him to get it if he wasn't ready. Then one day I put it down and he walked over to it and gave it a nudge, and that was massive progress.

Paddy was used to working a lot, so we began putting a saddle on his back, but we didn't actually make him do anything. It was just so he could get used to it and know that we weren't going to force him to do anything he didn't want to. It was so we could ease him into everything, and give him time to get used to the fact that his new life was going to be very different.

He was very wild and it took a long time for him to calm down. Even now, his early trauma means he frightens very easily. Paddy hated men for years, although he is better with them now, and he hates hearing raised voices. If he hears any kind of shouting I have to go and soothe him as he gets so scared.

It took him a year to build up the confidence to interact with us. He'd go round the entire length of the field to avoid us – it was so sad. I knew I had to just treat him as kindly as I could and leave him until he was ready.

Badger was great with him and he helped to build up his confidence by being by his side day and night. It was like he was mentoring him. He was so caring and if Paddy had food on his face Badger would lick it off. Paddy also stumbled when he walked sometimes, and Badger would stop and wait for him to catch up with him. He was so patient. A couple of times Paddy managed to get his leg stuck in the fence, and Badger waited with him until one of us arrived. He wouldn't leave his side and he'd reassure him by nudging him while we were trying to free him. It was the sweetest thing.

Paddy still has his moments where he gets spooked so it's a case of constantly reassuring him. I don't mind that he'll never be 'normal'. Some people think it's not safe for me to be around him but I know his ways and I've got such a strong bond with him. I trust him completely. I do training with him, which he enjoys, and I give him a lot of love. We're good for each other.

I didn't ride Paddy for several more years until he was completely ready, which was as it should be. It coincided with Badger's retirement so it worked perfectly. Badger had got too old to be ridden and he now enjoys a relaxing life in the field hanging out with his mates.

Though I love the company of animals, I was still quite an outgoing little girl and very chatty, and I still am. I always wanted to try new things and I could drive a quad bike by the time I was five. I enjoyed nursery and school, although I was always getting into trouble. I wasn't naughty and I didn't wind people up or anything, but I talked a lot so I was always being told to pipe down by the teachers.

My primary school was about ten minutes down the road from my first house and there were only ten children in my class because I come from such a small area. The only time I noticed my school was a bit different was when I was older and we went to play games against other schools. We used to have borrow their players to make up our team! There were so many of them, it seemed really unfamiliar and odd. The nice thing was that everyone in my school knew each other and it was a very close-knit environment, but it also meant the teachers could watch your every move. *That's* probably why I got in trouble!

I went to a high school that was about twenty minutes away from home and I used to share a minibus with some of the other kids. There still were only around three hundred pupils in the entire school so things felt quite small.

Because I spent so much time with the horses I guess I didn't do a lot of things that your average teenager does. I was constantly mucking out and tending to the horses while all my friends were going out shopping or meeting for lunch. I was never going to be that teenager who went to loads of parties or pubs and clubs. But do I feel like I missed out on anything? Honestly, not at all. I'm not a hugely sociable person and it may sound strange to some people but I've always preferred spending time with my animals. Growing up, I'd only really spent time with my friends when we were at school, and I was never one of those kids who would phone their friends up for a chat as soon as I got in. I'd be straight out in the field with the horses, or out playing with our dogs.

I still have lots of the same friends I had at school but really I'm at heart a bit of a hermit. I'm naturally a bit of a loner so it never crosses my mind to think, I must organise a bit of a meet up with everyone this weekend.

My friends love going out, especially now a lot of them are at university, but it's not the life for me. For so long I thought there was something wrong with me and I'd question whether I was boring. But at the end of the day, you've got to do what makes you happy.

I'm a real hermit and I would much rather be at home. Even now my friends will organise a night out and I'll think to myself, 'Do I have to go? Is it essential?' I really only ever go to catch up my friends, not for the drinking. I'd much rather go round to someone's house and spend time with just that one person so we can have a proper catch up, rather than shouting over loud music (I realise I sound about a hundred).

Don't get me wrong, I do have a bit of a social life, but it's a very small one. I like going to the gym, spending time with my pets and being outside in the fresh air. I would rather do that than get dressed up and go into town to get drunk any day. If I meet up with my friends we'll go for tea and cake or round to each other's houses for dinner. I very rarely go 'out out', unless it's to an event that's to do with the horses.

The nearest big town to where I live is Darlington and that's got a lot of shops and restaurants, but it was too far away for us to be able to get to on our own when I was growing up. Sometimes I'd see groups of teenage girls on TV or on social media going out on a Saturday night and wonder if I should be doing the same, but I've never been into alcohol or going clubbing. I used to look up to celebrities and think I wanted their glamorous party lifestyles but as I got older I realised that actually, I'm really happy with my own life.

Because I was always a bit of a tomboy and loved being outdoors so much it seemed natural that I chose to study farming at school. We had a working farm on the school grounds where we could learn how everything worked. The group was made up entirely of boys apart from me and my best mate, Kim. We learnt about lambing and how to milk a cow, and we all loved being around animals so we had lots in common. We'd feed the chickens, collect the hens' egg and milk the goats – all typical farming stuff, I guess.

We were the only school in the UK running that programme at the time, but it's not available anymore because it's not seen as a qualification, which I think is a real shame. I'd love if it other school kids had the same opportunities we had because I think it was one of the most important parts of my education.

It was also the course the class troublemakers were put on so they could be taught about discipline and hard work, and it made a huge difference to them. There were a couple of boys who totally turned things around for themselves while they were doing the course because they finally found something they really enjoyed doing. And, more importantly, something they were good at. Nothing is better for self-esteem than being good at something you love.

When it came to my love of horses, obviously my

mates from pony club were just like me, but I think some of the other kids at school thought it was odd that I was so obsessed with animals. I had a horse pencil case, notebook, pen and bag – you name it. Most of my mates were more interested in boys and music so we'd talk about those things when we were together too. I didn't talk about horses all the time, honest. A lot of the girls at school were also into hair and make-up and they weren't big interests of mine either. Even now it's rare for me to dress up, and if I'm hanging out with the horses the most I'll have on is a bit of lip balm. You'll be lucky if I've brushed my hair.

As you've probably worked out, horses were definitely my main focus growing up, but I also loved playing football with the boys in our local park every Sunday. I've always been tall (I'm six feet now) so I had the right physique for it. My dad was the manager of the team so I played alongside my brother and I used to look forward to it all week. But then a new law banned girls who were under sixteen from playing with boys and I was absolutely gutted.

My long-term career plan was always to do something with animals. I really wanted to be a vet for a while but when I realised I absolutely hated the sight of blood – to the point where I wanted to pass out whenever I saw it! – I knew that wasn't going to work. A vet who doesn't like blood is like someone who can't swim wanting to be a lifeguard.

My backup plan was to be a writer but I was worried that my grammar wasn't good enough and my spelling was terrible. I wrote the idea off before realising down the line that spelling is the kind of thing you can get better at with a bit of dedication. If you've got a passion for something and a strong idea your writing doesn't have to be word perfect. That's what I've learnt, anyway. And isn't that what spellcheck on your computer is for?

Chapter 2

A Little Miracle

Even my friends who were into horses started to lose interest in them as they got older. They began talking about going out and their plans for college instead. I started to wonder if there was something wrong with me because I was still obsessed. All I wanted to do was spend time with Badger, Paddy and Pepper. Should I have been thinking about my future too?

Most of my mates were planning to stay on at my school's sixth form after our GCSEs to do A-levels. I was the only person in my year not go down that route and I did feel like the odd one out. Instead I decided to go to Richmond College, a forty-minute journey from home.

I chose A-levels in sport, hospitality, English language and drama, the latter because I went through a stage of thinking I wanted to be an actress. I got an A* in my drama GCSE so I wondered if it could be something I'd want to pursue. I was in all sorts of plays at school – everything from *Matilda* to *Titanic* – and I really enjoyed it, but acting is so competitive. Now I look back I don't think I had enough belief that I could make it.

I knew from the moment I walked through the doors of Richmond College that we weren't a match made in heaven. After being at such tiny schools all my life it felt massive. I'd been used to three hundred pupils, whereas Richmond College had three thousand of them, and they all seemed way cooler and more worldly than me. The minute I got there I felt overwhelmed and lost.

When I woke up on my second day dreading the thought of going, I knew in my heart I'd made the wrong decision. I really wanted to give Richmond a decent go, but even the location was all wrong – it was such a long journey. I didn't get home until it was getting dark, which meant I didn't have very long to spend with the horses. By day four I hated it so much I sat my parents down and told them I was going to drop out. If I didn't like it after four days, imagine how much I would have hated it after two years. I'm such a home girl so I thought the college that was closer would suit me better. But, as it turns out, I didn't enjoy that either.

I left Richmond and, as I'd done so early on in the term, I managed to join Wensleydale College, the sixth form at my old school, where all my friends were. I began studying for a BTEC in sport because I had fallen in love with the idea of becoming a riding instructor. I liked college, but even though I was happier at Wensleydale, the bottom line was that I wasn't really suited to the college life at all. I wanted to be outside with my animals, not in a classroom. I felt like I was going through the motions and truthfully, I was only going to college because it was what was expected of me. You have to try and find your place in the world and sixteen is very young to decide what you want to do with the rest of your life. Sometimes the only way to know you don't want to do something is by trying it.

Despite that, I didn't want to look like a total dropout so I decided to stick with my course for a while longer and hope I magically started to love it.

My classmates were really nice and we got to do some interesting things but something in me kept telling me it wasn't the right path. The minute college finished for the day I'd run home and see the horses and that's when I felt most content. I kept thinking to myself, if only there was a way I could make money from doing what I love most – being around my horses. But those kinds of jobs didn't exist, did they?

By November 2012, I'd been at college for nearly four months and I was finding it increasingly difficult to feel enthusiastic about what I was doing. On top of everything my course was very active and, not surprisingly, it involved a lot of sport, and I started to experience a lot of pain in my lower back when we were running or playing team games. My brother had experienced quite bad growing pains when he was growing up so I put it down to the same thing and carried on as best I could, but sometimes I was in agony and there were a few times when I had to sit classes out.

It was all quite frustrating, but little did I know someone, or rather something, was about to come into my life and change it for ever . . .

*

One day I was up at the field feeding the horses when a lady called Caroline, who owned a breeder's yard down the road, pulled up in her car and called me over. She said to me, 'I've got too many horses at the moment and I need to rehome some of them. I've got a little Shetland who's six months old. He's smaller than normal because he's got dwarfism so I can't breed from him. Would you like him?'

When Caroline lowered her hand to the ground to show how little the Shetland was I kind of didn't believe her. How could a horse be that small? It didn't make sense! Without even thinking I said, 'Yes, why not?' I didn't even stop to consider, is this a good idea? Have I got too many animals? What will my parents say? It just felt like the right thing to do.

Caroline invited me over to meet this little horse, so I walked over to her stables a few days later. She took me to the paddock and I was so shocked when I saw this little thing I started laughing. He was a tiny, hairy mess, standing in the middle of a flooded field on his own. I looked at him with his scruffy hair and little legs and thought, *what on earth is that?* The field was so boggy he'd sunk down so he looked even shorter than he actually was. I could barely see his legs.

I was totally taken aback. He started running around and, despite being such a scruff, my main thought was, *oh my god, he's so cute*. Foals always have really curly coats, and he hadn't been brushed for a long time so he looked like something out of an old rock band! Coupled with a really long mane this was one small, shaggy pony – he reminded me of Sully from *Monsters, Inc.*

I fell totally in love with him and there was no doubt about whether I was taking him. I couldn't believe anyone could bear to give something so beautiful away. I think it was love at first sight for both of us.

Breeders usually wait until Shetlands are fully matured – about two or three years old – before they sell them. Sometimes breeders will wait until they're even older and have done some showing in competitions, and it's also common for them to wait until they've stopped teething. When horses are teething they can get a bit nibbly and because breeders want to hold on to their good reputation they won't let them go if there's a risk of them biting someone!

*

Of course, this adorable little pony was my Little Alf. This is what I imagine his life story before he met me had been: Alfie was born in a field on a bright, sunny April day in 2012 and when he first appeared no one realised there was anything different about him. His mum would have been pregnant for eleven months and then gone into labour. Like all mums, she would have been in a lot of pain so she would have lain on the ground while she prepared to give birth. Usually horses only have one foal at a time, and sadly if by chance they do have two one often dies.

Sometimes horses are given antibiotics to help when they foal out (give birth), but because Alfie was so small I imagine his mum would have had a really easy birth. The yard probably had no idea Alf was going to be any different to other horses while his mum was pregnant. She would have looked just as big as pregnant horses usually do.

Once Alf was born his mum would have cleaned him and then waited for him to get up on his own. Foals have to be up and standing within forty minutes or there's a chance there's something wrong with them. It's a bit like how everyone knows a human baby is OK because it cries. After they've found their feet, foals should be walking and feeding from their mum within the first two hours. The mum and foal bond really quickly so Alf would have felt very safe and secure. Foals generally live off their mum's milk for the first six months to a year until they're weaned, but they also eat hay or grass from the day they're born. Knowing how greedy Alf is he probably ate anything he could get his little teeth on.

Generally, horses that are born at a breeder's yard will be sold. It's not a case of breeding them and then keeping them for pets or anything, if a horse is kept it will be for breeding off it. Breeders have to build up a reputation for producing good quality horses, which they can sell for thousands of pounds. For instance, if I built up my Russell name and I became known for breeding healthy, beautiful horses, people would then know they were getting a quality thoroughbred horse if they bought one from me.

Yards typically consist of stables and loads of land, and sometimes the horses are left out in a field rather than being in stables. The yard where we got Pepper was purely fields so all the horses would breed and foal out in the fields, which basically means the babies are born in the mud. Shetlands are very hardy so it's not a problem to leave them out all year round, but that would never happen to an expensive racehorse.

Elite yards will have more facilities so they probably get sofas and satellite TV in their stables.

The yard where Alf was living was specifically for Shetlands, which are generally sold as pets or for kids to ride. People also show them at competitions as they're such beautiful-looking animals, but they're never used as racehorses because they just don't have the speed. If Alf had been born standard size it's possible he would have been kept and used for breeding, or sold on once he'd reached maturity.

One little-known fact about Shetlands is that because they're so intelligent, sometimes miniature ones are trained as guide horses and do the same job as guide dogs. They're also known to be good-natured, gentle, brave, impatient, forceful and cheeky, which basically describes Alf to a T.

Both parents have to have the dwarfism gene in order for it to be passed on to their foals, so Alfie's mum and dad must have carried it. Seventy-five per cent of the time the gene will be passed on to their offspring. Needless to say, because those carrying the gene are often culled, it's very rare to come across a Shetland with dwarfism. The most common traits in horses with dwarfism, apart from obviously being very small, are big heads, potbellies and misaligned

47

teeth. I'm lucky because Alfie has a real mild case of dwarfism so it doesn't affect his health too much.

Alf's mum and dad now live together in Boroughbridge, which is about an hour from me. I'm in contact with their new owners because when I released my first Alf magazine they happened to buy a copy and read all about Alf! They sent me an email telling me that they care for Alf's parents now, which was so lovely to hear. I had been worried about what had happened after they had Alf – they couldn't be used for breeding any more. There's such a strong chance they would have had another foal with dwarfism that the breeder wouldn't have taken the risk. Alf's dad would have been gelded immediately and then they both would have been 'retired', which can mean many things, and we're not talking slippers by the fire and *Countdown* on repeat.

Even successful racehorses that can't compete anymore and end up being sold on will be slaughtered. When I was fourteen I heard about a girl who decided she didn't want her horse anymore so he was 'sent away'. I just don't know how people can do that. Even now people think I'm mad because I've still got the first pony I ever had, but I would never send an animal to its death just because it doesn't suit my needs anymore. I guess that's why I end up with so many waifs and strays.

When I first saw him, Alf was the same size as he is now. He grew like any normal foal to start with, and then because of his dwarfism he promptly stopped. The breeders realised he was different when he was about four months old because it was obvious he wasn't growing as he should have been. As well as being smaller than usual Caroline would have noticed that his legs were wonky and his ears weren't growing.

Because he wasn't 'perfect' Alf started to be rejected by the rest of the horses, including his own mum at times. He was still getting milk from her but she wasn't giving him the attention he needed. Because of that he had to be weaned earlier than he normally would have been. He wasn't being groomed properly or socialised with other horses. The other horses could sense that there was something wrong with him so they didn't want to interact with him. I like to think that Alf wasn't too aware of it because it upsets me to think that he felt like he wasn't good enough, because he is. He's more than good enough.

*

So there was Alfie, looking so unhappy with his little legs stuck in the mud that all I wanted to do was run over and give him a big hug. I wanted to rescue him so he could live a long, happy life.

Despite being desperate to, I couldn't take him away with me that day because Caroline had to make sure he was fully weaned before he left the yard. But she said she'd let me know when he was ready to go. I was so excited. I did feel guilty about taking him away from his mum, but all things considered it was the best case scenario. I didn't even want to think about what might happen if I didn't take him. His breeders would have found someone else to take him, shot him, or sent him to slaughter for dog meat. I know, it's really not nice to think about.

When I got back home that afternoon I didn't say anything to my parents about our new addition. I was too scared they might have said I couldn't adopt him and that would have broken my heart. But I'd already got so many other animals, what harm could another one do? I had been thinking about getting another pony at some point in the future anyway, though I definitely hadn't expected to end up with a handbag horse. When my parents asked me what I'd been doing that day I replied, 'Oh, not much!' but I kept thinking, I've got a big secret. I felt terrible not telling them the truth but I wanted to enjoy the idea of that messy ball of fluff coming to live with us just a little while longer.

The following day I went out and bought a little head collar (basically a lead that goes over the horse's head) for my scruffy new Shetland and hid it in my wardrobe. Then I waited patiently for Caroline to phone and let me know when I could pick him up. I didn't hear anything for over two weeks and I started to get really worried that she'd given him away to someone else. I would have been so devastated. I imagined, because I was only sixteen, she might have wanted an adult to look after him instead, and just thinking about it made me feel gutted.

Finally, after four very long weeks, Caroline phoned on Christmas Eve to say I could collect my new horse that day. I was so relieved she still wanted me to have him, but there was a big problem – I still hadn't told my family my secret. It was going to be very hard to keep him to myself all Christmas, but I was willing to take my chances. That day Dad and John were out at a football match and my mum was out doing some last-minute Christmas shopping, so I knew I'd at least be able to sneak him into my field without anyone seeing. I'd deal with the fallout later.

I pretty much skipped all the way down to Caroline's stables because I was so eager to see Alf again. I walked straight over to his field and as soon as he spotted me he trotted over and swished his head. As I mentioned, he'd hardly had any human contact before so it was peculiar that he was so confident around me. I realise this will probably sound a bit crazy but it was like we had some kind of connection. I think he knew I was coming to take him to a lovely new home.

I lobbed his head collar over him using a lasso technique that I'd perfected thanks to years of looking after my other horses (I'm not going to lie, it does look cool) and then he followed me calmly out of the gate. Caroline was really taken aback because he'd never experienced a halter before but he was totally at ease and happy to walk with me.

Because Alf was so small we were able to transport him back to my field in the back of Caroline's Land Rover. Once we managed to get him in there. Getting him to walk was one thing but getting him to climb into the back of a car was quite another. In the end I had to pick him up with Caroline's help, and we plonked him on the back seat.

Once he was in he seemed pretty happy. As we drove off, he poked his head through the two front seats like a dog. He was moving his head from side to side and watching what was going on out of the windscreen. It was his first real experience of the world outside of his field and he seemed fascinated. He also kept nuzzling my arm and pulling at my clothes. Considering he'd never been in a car before he was very relaxed. Every time I looked at him I had a massive smile on my face. He was just adorable. I was over the moon with my early Christmas present.

When we arrived at my field I opened the door of the car and he jumped out on his own, like a dog would. He didn't need, or ask for, my help! He looked around at his surroundings, took it all in and screamed really loudly as if he was letting everyone know he'd arrived. He was swishing his head around and whinnying. A lot of it was probably false bravado because he was somewhere that was completely unfamiliar, but he put on a good show of being brave.

Because of his age Alf was starting to get his stallion tendencies and I knew it was a bit of a risk to put him in the field with my other horses, but felt I had no other option. I also thought that having been on his own so much it was probably time for him to stand on his own four feet and get used to socialising.

I led him down to the field and when I opened the gate he trotted in and then turned round to look at me as if to say, 'What on earth are you doing?' My other horses didn't react terribly well either. They're all geldings (which means they'd had the snip and he hadn't!) and Alf suddenly got this surge of confidence so started strutting around the field with his tail in the air, thinking he owned the place. Badger, Paddy and Pepper had been living together for a long time so they were used to each other and they got on really well – they must have thought this funny little thing was totally invading their territory.

Alf was parading up and down the field loving life, thinking he was amazing, but the other horses were so unimpressed. They kept raising their heads and snorting at him, but Alf didn't seem to care. What he lacked in height he certainly made up for in bravado.

On the positive side, Alf absolutely loved being in such a big field. He was in his element with all that space and long grass, and because it wasn't water-logged he was able to run around freely. (I swear I actually saw him smile at one point.)

I was standing by the gate watching him for ages. He kept coming over and nudging me and wanting attention, and I thought he was hilarious. After about an hour of posturing and trying to stamp his authority Alf decided he wanted to be friends with his field mates. But he had a bit of a battle on his hooves because every time he ran up to them to try and play they stared down at him with really angry looks on their faces. Not that it stopped Alf doing it time and time again, mind you. He's a brave chap, and even now he likes winding the other horses up when he's in the mood for it.

I could see that Badger, Paddy and Pepper were getting a bit tetchy, so I decided it was best to keep him away from them for a short time so they had a chance to get used to him.

I made him a special pen next to the field using some horse tape and flower pots (it was all a bit *Blue Peter*), and after a lot of persuasion I managed to coax him in to it. He seemed to settle in OK and trotted around happily and I thought, *problem solved*. But the minute I turned my back to get him some hay he broke through the tape and went flying off.

He was running around, making these crazy noises and I could see the other horses were getting annoyed again so I belted over to try and catch him. I'm so glad no one was around to see me because in trying to get hold of this tiny escapee I fell over three times and was covered in mud. On top of that every time I got near him he dashed off again so I looked completely ridiculous chasing him around. He, meanwhile, was having the time of his life.

After running around in circles for about ten minutes he walked over to the side of the field and stood still. I knew this was my opportunity to wrestle back some control. I tiptoed over, really stealthily, proud of how cunning I was being, but just as I was about to try and get his head collar on him he started running at full pelt towards the back of the field. He sped up as he got to the fencing and then dived underneath it on his knees. There was a little bridge at the bottom of the field which he sped right over and disappeared into the woods at a surprisingly fast pace for a horse with such tiny legs.

As I ran after him I was so panicked – all I could think was, I've only just got him and I've already lost him! The woods are huge, about twenty acres, so I had no idea how I'd ever find him. What if I never got him back? I couldn't bear to think about it.

I sprinted breathlessly into the trees and started

searching everywhere. Eventually I managed to find Alf standing in the middle of a path looking very shady. I think he'd shocked himself with his naughty behaviour. The only reason he hadn't run any further was because there were loads of trees in the way blocking him, so goodness knows what would have happened if they hadn't been there.

I think he was quite worn out so I had an advantage, and after a bit of a tussle I managed to get his head collar on. Success! But then he flatly refused to move. He hadn't had any halter training, which meant he'd never walked on a lead before that day, and no matter how much I tried to talk him round or pulled on his head collar nothing could persuade him to budge. So much for being so good earlier on. This was still a wild stallion who definitely knew his own mind. He may have been small, but he was very mighty.

I decided to try bribing him with some carrots and mints that were in my coat pocket, but because he'd never eaten anything like that before he was very suspicious of them. He'd lean forward and sniff them and then turn his nose up.

So there I was, standing in the middle of a huge wood with Little Alf, wondering how on earth I was going to get him to move. And also where I was going to take him once I *had* got him moving. I had to keep him somewhere safe, and I knew that if I put him back in the field he wouldn't be welcomed by the other horses. And even worse, he now knew how to escape, so chances were he'd soon be off exploring again.

It came to me that my friend Diane had a stable nearby where she kept a lot of racehorses. I knew it was really secure but I wasn't sure if she'd have room for another horse, even if Alf was less than half the size of one of her regular tenants. I phoned Diane on my mobile and said, 'I know this is a bit weird but can I bring my new pony to stay with you? He's escaped from my field because he's small enough to get under the fencing.'

She was silent for a few seconds and then she laughed and said, 'What do you mean he got under the fencing? How can a horse be that little?'

I explained about Alf's dwarfism and she said, 'He sounds wonderful. I've got a spare stable so bring him round whenever you're ready.'

I was ready, but it didn't seem that Alf was. After much persuasion we started to make our way there. Very, very slowly.

Diane's stables were only a five-minute walk from the woods but, and I'm honestly not exaggerating, the journey ended up taking me eight and a half hours. Alf kept stopping and sitting down because we were walking on an unmade road and his little hooves kept slipping on the stones. Although he was small, he was pretty sturdy and heavy, so it wasn't like I could carry him like I had when I'd got him into Caroline's car. I was stuck! Every time we walked more than twenty paces he'd refuse to move any further. The more I pulled on his lead rope the more he resisted. Helpful.

We'd had loads of storms over the previous few days so the road was littered with puddles. Alf couldn't walk through most of them because they were too deep so he ended up swimming through them instead. I'd help him navigate his way through any big ones we came across, but just as I'd start to think we were making progress he'd decide he needed another rest.

Alf had never seen roads, let alone cars, until that morning so whenever a car drove by he'd get spooked. He'd back up to the fence and sit on his bottom like a dog. It was a true case of two hooves forward, one hoof back. People kept stopping their cars to look at him, tell me how cute he was, and take photos of him, which was nice, though – and little did I know, a sign of things to come!

I did my best to be understanding because it must have been very daunting for Alf. He was a blank canvas. All he'd known in his life so far was a field, and now he was experiencing big hunks of metal zooming past him and being pulled along a road by a girl he barely knew.

I tried to encourage him to move with carrots and apples again but he'd just stare at me. At one point I gave up too and I leant against one of the drystone walls, waiting for him to decide what his next move would be. I did have a moment when I thought, *how difficult is he going to be in the future if he's already like this?*

Alf and I started walking at midday and didn't get to the yard until gone eight p.m. Diane had already left for the day so I called her and let her know we'd arrived, and that I was going to get Alf settled in.

It was pitch black, we were both soaking wet and freezing but once we got there Alf was desperate to investigate. It looked quite similar to his old yard so it must have been a bit confusing that none of the other horses he knew were there.

I got Alf into his stable, gave him some food and

water and made sure he was comfortable. I was worried he'd find it strange being in a new place but he was calmer than I expected. To be honest, I think, like me, he was just happy to be out of the hammering rain. Also, being in a stable was a novelty for him because he'd only ever lived outside. Even now he loves being cosy and warm in his own stable – it's like his own little house.

Because he'd been out in a field for so long and hadn't been looked after brilliantly his hair had become matted and dreadlocked. I got a grooming kit out and gave him a bit of a brush, which he loved. He kept cocking his head to the side and nudging me every time I stopped. But it wasn't all cuteness and cuddles. Every time I tried to brush his feet he'd pick the brush up with his teeth and lob it across the stable. He still does it to this day, it's become one of his many tricks.

I ended up having to cut the dreadlocks out of Alfie's hair, and he still gets them now. I have to cut his hair every other day to make sure it doesn't get matted, otherwise it becomes a much bigger grooming job!

Alf was very tired and I knew he'd need a long sleep to get his energy back. He'd had such a big day leaving his old home, escaping from his new field, and then walking for hours to another new home. After all of that it must have been overwhelming for him to be in this new place. I didn't know how he would react to being on his own. He could hear the other horses but was separated from them and I was worried he'd feel anxious when I left.

I sat with him for ages to make sure he was OK. He kept leaning over and resting his head on me and sniffing me. He was so affectionate and it felt like we already had this strong connection. I loved being with him so much that I'd already forgiven him for his naughty antics that day.

I hated leaving Alf but the alternative was to sleep in the stable with him all night but my parents still didn't know about him, so that would be difficult to explain. It would have been a bit odd if I'd disappeared and then I'd rolled in the next morning freezing, hungry and covered in hay. And obviously very worrying!

Eventually I had to drag myself away. I made sure Alf was comfortable and then headed home. As I was walking I kept thinking, I can't believe I've got another horse. And one that's no bigger than my dog!

By the time I got home from settling Little Alf

in, my mum was back from shopping. She'd been worried because she'd been trying to get hold of me for ages but my phone had run out of battery. When she asked where I'd been I replied, 'Just out with the horses,' which was kind of true. I felt so guilty but I didn't think it was the right time to say, 'Oh, I've just been hanging with my new miniature pony!'

It may sound like an odd thing to say but I really missed Alf that night. I was bursting to tell my family all about him but I needed to wait for the right time. It was Christmas the following day and they had other things on their minds. For the first time ever presents weren't the thing I was most excited about. I just couldn't wait to go to bed so I could get up and spend more time with Little Alf.

Chapter 3

Alf's Big Arrival

When the next morning finally dawned, I rushed the rest of the family to open our Christmas presents early and then got myself dressed to go to feed Badger, Paddy and Pepper. And then, of course, I slipped away to see Alf. I always went to see the horses on Christmas Day so my parents didn't suspect a thing.

As soon as I walked through the door of his stable Alf looked over at me and whinnied. It was like he'd been waiting for my arrival. I was just as excited to see him as he was to see me.

I took him outside so he could have a look around the yard in the light and he soon made his mark. Whenever one of the horses made any noise he'd join in with them, he wasn't in the least bit intimidated. In fact, when I took him for a walk he dragged me towards a field where a group of horses were grazing and then started nipping them and diving under their feet. It was like he was saying, 'Don't judge me on my appearance. I may be small but I'm in charge.' It didn't take long for him to think he ran the yard. He was, and still is, so bossy – Shetlands are known for being naughty but I do wonder if Alf is cheekier than most because of his size.

After Alf had made his presence known I went and fetched a wheelbarrow so I could clean up the area around his stable. He ran straight up to it and tried to push it over, and when it didn't topple the first time he battered it again and again. It was much bigger than him but that didn't faze him. I think he saw it as a challenge.

All that kept going round in my head was, what have I done? Was this really the best idea in the world? But he was so cute I batted all those feelings away.

When I got home I started to feel terribly guilty

about my big (little) secret, so I decided I couldn't keep it any longer. I figured I could probably just about get away with it, as it was Christmas! I announced to my parents that I had a present for them but they'd have to come to Diane's stables to see it. They both looked very confused. My dad laughed and said, 'I hope it's not another horse!' I laughed along, slightly panicking inside.

We all put on our coats and walked up to the yard. I opened the gate and Alf instantly started whinnying when he heard me coming. I took Mum and Dad over to his stable and they both poked their heads around the side of his stable door. I'm sure at that point they were convinced it was a horse, but the look on their faces when they saw who was on the other side of the door was priceless. 'This is Alf!' I smiled nervously.

There was a small part of me that was worried my parents would tell me I couldn't keep him, but like me they're pretty soft. Plus, we already had loads of pets so what harm was one more? Mum and Dad have always said I can have as many pets as I like as long as I divide my time between them equally.

I explained that Alf needed a home and so I'd agreed to take him in, and I waited nervously for their reaction. My dad paused for a minute and then said, 'Well, I suppose he'll be welcomed into the family then, won't he?' I almost cheered! And I could tell my mum was really happy as well. She's definitely as bad as me when it comes to animals, and she clearly thought Alf was gorgeous.

With everything agreed, we opened the door to let Alf out so my parents could meet him properly. After a quick hello – surprise, surprise – he galloped straight across a field. Because he's so small we couldn't see his legs in the long grass so he looked like he was gliding rather than running. He tried to do a loud whinny but the noise that came out sounded like a cross between a grunt and a donkey bray. We all burst out laughing and from that moment on my parents loved Little Alf every bit as much as I did. The fact it was Christmas may have helped . . .

My brother didn't meet Alf until Boxing Day because he was at home hanging out with the dogs on Christmas Day. I think he found him slightly ridiculous at first but they've become mates now – Alf's always playing with John's shoelaces and nipping his feet. That was also the first time my friend Diane met Alf. She's very practical and she's got racehorses so she was a bit like, 'What are you doing to do with him?' But she still thought he was very cute, and she was really supportive of me rescuing him.

My parents and I headed home and had Christmas dinner with my brother, and then I went back up to the yard in the afternoon to spend time with Alf and give him another brush. It was then that I noticed he hadn't touched his food or water. I took him out for a walk to make sure he was OK and he immediately started munching on grass. Then he pulled me over to a puddle and started lapping at the rainwater. He'd clearly never had horse food before, or drunk from a bowl.

When I took him back to his stable I put his water bowl down in front of him and he stared at me, then turned his back on it. It took me a week to teach him to drink from a bowl, and I had to feed him tiny amounts of food by hand until he got to grips with the fact that grass wasn't the only thing available to him. Now it's hard to stop him eating, but it was a real worry in those early days.

Because his arrival had been so quick and unexpected I didn't have time to buy Alf any Christmas presents so to make sure he didn't feel left out I shared some of my other horses' Christmas treats with him.

He didn't know what they were so he spat most of them out. The next time I went to see him I took a treat ball I'd bought for the dogs – I put some horse food inside and gave it to him instead. He started rolling it around and playing with it, and he seemed to be able to do really clever things with it. It got me thinking about what I may be able to teach him to do . . .

I invited some of my friends to visit him over the following few days and they thought he was amazing, though one of them did say to me, 'Why have you got another horse? What are you doing? You're never going to have any spare time!'

Alf's first real friend at the yard, once he'd stopped bullying the other horses, was a standard-sized Shetland called Teddy. He's a pretty big chap but he's very sweet with Alfie and they used to play together whenever they were both out in the ménage. Teddy already had his own gang but he took Alfie under his wing and looked after him. Even now they go for play dates together and they both scream with excitement when they see each other. If Teddy's owner goes away Teddy will come for a sleepover at our yard, which Alf loves.

*

That Christmas I got a really smart camera, a Nikon D3300, and I was over the moon because I love photography. I knew as soon as I opened it I was going to use Little Alf as my first model and I started taking photos of him straight away. I taught myself about the technical side of taking photos and how to edit pictures and I found myself really enjoying it.

I put a few of the photos up on my personal Instagram account and they got a really good response. Then I put some on my Facebook page and everyone loved Alf and left really nice comments about him. I already had my own Tumblr blog where I'd write about equestrian stuff (which is basically anything to do with horses), and slowly but surely I turned it into more of a Little Alf blog.

I started posting photos and I couldn't believe that within two weeks Alf had over a thousand followers. I thought I might as well see how far I could go with it. I had nothing to lose.

It took me a couple of weeks to get to grips with how to blog on Tumblr properly, but once I did Alf's followers started to grow steadily. I began to feel really hopeful that Alf would become well known, but if you'd told me back then it would lead to Alf and I having our own range of books and winning awards I would have thought you were crazy.

I looked up to loads of bloggers and YouTubers but I didn't have any idea I could emulate their careers. For a start I knew it could take a really long time to build up a following. And then one picture changed everything.

I posted a really cute picture of Alf and someone shared it, saying that he looked like a chicken nugget. I thought it was really funny and the next thing I knew it got forty thousand hits. It still trends to this day, and every time it gets posted we get more followers.

After that I set up an official Facebook page for Alf, and then dedicated Instagram, Twitter and YouTube accounts. I uploaded photos and videos with a bit of copy. People started messaging me, asking when I was going to post again. Back then I was writing the blog from Alf's point of view. He'd talk about me and give his opinion on things and the fact that people loved it made me feel so proud.

I did some funny things to get Alf noticed. I got him to pick up a box of Yorkshire Tea with his teeth (we do all genuinely drink it up here!). I put a picture of it up on Twitter and Yorkshire Tea retweeted it and sent us some free tea and a letter. It was so exciting that Alf was becoming so well known that big brands were taking notice.

Alf started to get genuine fans and I was shocked – I could never have imagined just how interested people would be in him. His followers quickly went into the thousands and when I'd see friends or family the first thing they'd say was 'how's Alf?', so I knew he was creating a stir.

When I went back to college in January I only had lessons in the morning so I'd go and see Badger, Paddy and Pepper straight afterwards and go for a ride on Paddy. Then I'd spend from two p.m. to four p.m. with Alf. Diane has got quite a big ménage so I'd take loads of photos of him while he skipped around in the sand. It was great for Alfie to be able to have fun while he was getting used to his new life. He changed so much in those first few weeks. He became even more confident, if you can believe it.

While Alf seemed really settled and content, I felt like I was totally in limbo. I was still cracking on with my college course, but I was really only doing it to fill time because I didn't know what else I could do. If I left college I'd have to get a full-time job, and I didn't feel ready for that either.

As January went on it was becoming more and more clear that my heart wasn't in college any more. I hated the thought of wasting two years doing something that didn't make me happy. I had some nice friends there but a few others started to say unkind things about my blog. That was hard to deal with because I felt like it was Alf they were being mean about. It would have been easier if they'd been taking the mickey out of me and not a 'stupid little horse', as someone put it. It didn't help that I'd also started doing some modelling, which also made me a prime target for bitchiness.

It seems so strange to think that I did modelling because it's not my kind of thing at all. I was always tall growing up, and then when I was fourteen I had a proper growth spurt and people started telling me I should try it. It never really appealed to me, but the more I looked into it the more I thought, *why not?*

When I was sixteen, a photographer who lives nearby asked if she could take some photos of me for her portfolio, and she decided to submit some of them to a few agencies in London. One of the agencies invited me down for a meeting, so I got the train down with my mum and they offered me a year-long contract.

I really didn't know what I was getting myself into. The first casting I attended was horrendous because it was so impersonal. Me and about fifty other girls were herded into this big room and I genuinely felt like an animal that was about to be sold at auction. The whole day made me feel really emotional because some of the other girls were so thin they were clearly unwell. It was upsetting to see how ill they looked. Obviously they wanted to be successful models so badly they thought it was worth risking their health. It didn't feel like my kind of world at all.

I got asked to go to more castings but my first experience put me off so much that whenever my agency asked me to go and try out for jobs I'd make excuses about why I couldn't make it. I was always put up for commercial work and brochures and I did force myself to a few more go-sees, but I always came out feeling really despondent. I guess to me the modelling world felt quite seedy, and I hated the fact I was being judged solely on how I looked. Sometimes casting directors wouldn't even bother to ask my name, let alone have a conversation with me. I'm not a particularly resilient character in situations like that, especially as I was so young. Rejection is tough, whatever form it comes in. I could see how the way I was being treated could be really damaging to my self-esteem long term.

I'd always been a happy person but the modelling meant that insecurities started to creep in. I started to doubt myself if I didn't get the jobs I went for, which was horrible. I really didn't want it to have a negative effect on my confidence. It just wasn't worth it. I was earning money but even that wasn't a great incentive because the way I was earning it was making me feel rubbish.

It wasn't all bad, though. One campaign was a *Black Swan*-style shoot, which was very cool, and I worked on some catalogue shoots with some really lovely people. I wasn't skinny enough for catwalk shows so I was never put up for castings for those. That was probably a good thing because knowing me I would have fallen over if I'd had to walk in heels.

The other issue was that I'd often get asked to go to London for castings on Saturday and that was my really important time with the horses, so it was a real wrench. I also got tired from all the travelling. Although I love London and really enjoyed the independence of going down there on my own, I was always much happier to get back home.

I also felt massive pressure when it came to my

weight. I had slimmed down to a size eight but your body naturally fills out at around fifteen or sixteen and I was finding it such a struggle to stay as small as was expected of me. I was constantly fighting against my body and I didn't want to put myself through that. I knew I couldn't be a person who worried about how I looked every day, or felt guilty about every tiny thing I put in my mouth. I love food and would be miserable if I was munching on a salad while my family were eating a lovely, hearty meal. My parents have always instilled in me that I should eat fruit and vegetables and avoid fizzy drinks and tons of sugar. Those are basic sensible food rules so I knew the right way to take care of myself. I just wasn't doing it very well at that time.

Also I wasn't eating as much as I should have been and that had a negative effect on my energy levels. I'm very much into the whole 'mind, body and soul' thing and I knew I wasn't looking after myself very well. I started exercising a lot more in a bid to lose weight, and I noticed that my back was becoming more painful than ever. My ribs also started to hurt. I put it all down to muscle aches from going to the gym so I didn't bother to go and see my doctor.

However, I'd been injured twice over the previous couple of years, both times while I was riding Badger, so I thought it could be connected to that. The first incident was when a Jack Russell started chasing Badger and he got scared. It was a really frosty morning and when Badger bucked I catapulted over his head and landed in a heap. When I stood up I was in so much pain. I knew I'd done something to my ribs because I couldn't breathe properly. I didn't go to hospital, which I probably should have done. It took me a year to properly get over it because I didn't get any kind of treatment, but I just kept thinking to myself, it'll be better soon. I assumed it would somehow be OK. Another time we were in the ménage doing jumps and when we got to a high jump Badger stopped dead. I fell off and landed really awkwardly, and for a few seconds I felt like I was paralysed. When I managed to get back on my feet, despite being relieved, I could hardly walk so I knew I'd done some serious damage.

I was always getting a bit bruised and battered because that's what happens when you ride, but both of those episodes were worrying. I had to play down how uncomfortable it was because I was concerned that my parents would stop me riding at all.

Because I hadn't ever been to get my injuries checked out I started to wonder if I'd done some lasting damage. My body started making strange clicking noises a lot and most worryingly it felt like my right hip was going in and out of the joint. I had so much going on with my animals, college and travelling to and from London I decided to wait and see if it righted itself, which in hindsight wasn't the most sensible decision I've ever made.

Some of my friends were really supportive about my modelling and were really happy for me. Then there were others who told me I was too fat to be a model, or said I was ridiculous for thinking I could make it. I got snide comments here and there, but I told myself that actually it said a lot more about them than it did about me. My male friends didn't even mention it because they weren't fussed. I guess there wasn't anything for them to feel competitive about.

Eventually the pressure became too much and I left my agency in London. I didn't feel in any way sad about that decision. It's probably one of the best I've ever made. I've since done some modelling for local companies and my experiences have all been great because the people involved haven't expected me to look like I live on a diet of steamed vegetables and air. They were all very kind to me and happy with the way I looked so that gave me my confidence back. No one was telling me I had to change; I was enough just as I was.

I still do modelling here and there, and I've done a lot for an equestrian brand called Tottie, which is great because I can do it with Alfie. So Alf is a model too now!

It was late January 2014 that something happened which had a dramatic effect on my future.

My college class were supposed to go caving in Ingleton as part of our BTEC course. Caving involves crawling on your belly underground in really confined areas until you reach huge open spaces. Often these massive areas are filled with stalactites and they're really breathtaking. I'd been caving loads of times before so I wasn't worried about it at all, even though it can be dangerous if the conditions aren't right.

The morning of the excursion dawned, but it had been raining a lot the day before so the caves were flooded, and Mum told me in no uncertain terms that I wasn't allowed to go. So many people have accidents in the caves, and it's even been known for people to die down there in extreme conditions. The caves can flood in a matter of minutes so if it had rained again that day the whole group could easily have become trapped. It wasn't just my mum who felt that way – my college decided to change the day's activity to kayaking to be on the safe side. I wasn't bothered, I loved kayaking so was happier not to take the risk of being trapped underground . . .

We travelled to Lake Semerwater, a glacial lake in North Riding. Lake Semerwater is an incredible place. It's so beautiful – there was snow on the tops of the hills and the view was stunning.

Legend goes that there used to be a village where the lake is now. It's said that hundreds of years ago a beggar visited the village asking for food and shelter but he was turned away from every house. Eventually he found a couple in a small cottage on the outskirts who were willing to take him in. The following morning he cursed the village and said, 'Semerwater rise, Semerwater sink, and bury the town, all save the house where they gave me meat and drink.' According to the story, the lake rose up and flooded the entire village and everyone living there died – apart from the couple who had shown the beggar kindness. Even now, people say the village still exists at the bottom of the lake. It's one of those stories that's been passed down the generations, so who knows if it's true?

There's a massive rock in the lake, and according to another legend, that came about because a giant and the devil had an argument and threw rocks at each other and one landed slap bang in the middle. Both stories sound a little far-fetched, but they've made Semerwater a big tourist attraction and it's a fascinating place.

As soon as we were given our boating safety talk we all got into our waterproof clothes and climbed into our kayaks. The first hour was amazing, but when we turned back to head towards shore something went wrong. The wind was against me and I was fighting to keep control of my kayak. The gusts were throwing me around all the over the place and I had to use all of my strength to stay on course.

A big blast of wind must have caught hold of my boat and while the rest of the group went one way, I went the other. Though the instructor was shouting instructions to me, because the wind was howling I found it was impossible to hear him. I was paddling as fast as I could to try to get back to the group, but I couldn't steer the kayak straight. I've always been active so I've got pretty good upper body strength, but nothing I was doing was working.

I started drifting further and further away from the rest of the class and I could feel my breathing speeding up as I started to panic. Just when I thought things couldn't get any worse I realised one of my feet had somehow become caught underneath one of the pedals at the bottom of the boat. It was impossible to reach down and free it so all I could do was wiggle it around in the hope it released. I was so distracted that I didn't notice my kayak was rocking violently from side to side, and before I had a chance to steady it, it tipped upside down.

I don't remember actually hitting the water and the first few seconds after I fell in were a total blur, but I remember struggling to try and get out of the boat. Whatever I did, I wasn't able to manoeuvre myself out because my foot was still caught up.

I knew I needed to get my head above water but I was completely trapped. I started to really panic and think the worst. The water was bitterly cold and I knew that if I couldn't free my foot I had no chance of getting my kayak back up the right way. The rest of the group were still a good distance away so I didn't even know if anyone had seen what had happened.

All I could do was pray that someone had spotted me and would come to my rescue.

Somehow – and to this day I have no idea how – I managed to rotate my kayak so I was above the surface. Both of my shoes were in the bottom of the boat – I must have kicked them off in the struggle.

I don't know if I've blocked everything because it was so traumatic, but I only remember small snippets of what happened next. Once I was upright, I was gasping for air and lightheaded from the lack of oxygen. I felt like I was going to pass out and was so cold I could barely feel my body. I looked around to see if anyone was coming to help me and I saw an instructor rushing over. He pulled me across onto his boat and paddled us back to the shore.

At that point I went into some kind of shock. I was shaking and although I didn't realise it at the time I was in the early stages of hyperthermia. The whole incident only lasted about five minutes but everything felt like it was going in slow motion, meaning it seemed to go on for ages.

The instructor asked me what had gone wrong and I explained that my foot had got stuck. He looked at the pedals in my kayak. For some reason one of the bars had turned the wrong way.

The rest of my classmates were out of the water by then and they were asking me if I was OK, but I was shaking so much I couldn't speak. I took my wet jumper off and one of my friends gave me her dry one so I could try and warm up a bit.

My right wrist was aching and the instructor explained that sometimes you can suffer from what's known as 'kayaking wrist', where they become really sore from using the paddles. My teacher wrapped both of my hands up and then it was time to head back to college.

It took about half an hour for everyone to get back on the minibus and I was still shaking. As the journey went on my hands started to turn blue and I was as white as a ghost. Friends gave me more clothes to put on but no matter what I did I couldn't get warm.

As soon as we arrived at college I got a hot drink and sat by a radiator but I still felt really unwell, which I put down to swallowing lots of lake water. The school rang my mum and she came to pick me up, and when she arrived I was really tearful. My teacher suggested that my mum take me straight to the doctor but all I wanted to do was go home.

As soon as we got in Mum made me a cup of tea and I had a hot bath. I was expecting it to thaw me out but I came out feeling just as cold. I sat in front of the fire in our living room but I was in so much pain I had to lie on my side and curl my body up. My whole body was aching and my lower back was throbbing constantly.

The following day Mum took me to the doctor to get my wrists re-wrapped. I was also given some antibiotics because, on top of everything else, I'd managed to pick up an infection from the water. I didn't go into college the following day because I still wasn't feeling well.

My parents watched me like a hawk and told me I had to spend the weekend relaxing. That would be a dream come true for a lot of people, but I found it really hard because I always like to be doing something.

I started to feel better by Sunday so I went riding to take my mind off everything. Paddy and I set off but after a few minutes I started to feel really severe pain in my lower back again so I had to cut the ride short. The aching got worse over the next few days, to the point where it hurt whenever I bent over. The pain even started to wake me up in the night. There was no ignoring it this time.

Chapter 4

Ball Games

I told my parents about my back pain and they told me I had to go and get it checked out straight away. Mum came along to the appointment and as soon as my doctor examined my lower back he said he could feel that something definitely wasn't right. It was swollen and he looked very concerned.

I'd gone along expecting him to tell me I'd overexerted myself and send me home with some stretches to do – I thought I was just being a bit of a wimp. Then he mentioned the word 'hospital' and I looked at Mum in horror. My doctor said it was essential I got checked out properly so they could get to the bottom of what was going on. He said he couldn't say for sure what it was but it was possible it could be linked to the falls I'd had in the past.

As we were driving home Mum said to me, 'Please don't panic. If there is something wrong they'll be able to sort it out. We're all here for you and everything will be OK.' It was exactly what I needed to hear, but I couldn't help but still be very worried.

I was referred for an MRI scan and when the hospital called me after two days to say they could see me in a week I didn't think it was a great sign. The fact I was being seen so quickly made me think that my doctor was seriously alarmed.

My dad drove me to the James Cook University Hospital in Middlesbrough and I went inside one of those giant round tubes so they could scan my entire body. The MRI lasted for about forty minutes and the whole time I was in the buzzing donut I was thinking about all the different things that could be wrong with me. It was sending me a bit crazy. I'm also not a fan of small spaces but I knew it was all for the best.

You're supposed to take all of your metal off before

you have an MRI. I still had my jeans on and I forgot that my top button was made of brass. It got really hot and started to burn my belly and when the nurse asked if I was OK I said, 'No, my button is burning!' He couldn't hear what I was saying above the humming of the machine so just replied, 'Oh good!' I had a little burn mark afterwards but it wasn't anything too dramatic.

I had to wait three weeks for the results and I thought about what they would say every single day. If people stood near me when my back clicked they could hear it so they'd ask me what was wrong. It was hard to get it out of my head. I was still at college but I couldn't join in with any of the sporting activities so I spent the weeks watching from the sidelines wondering if I'd ever be able to do all the things I took for granted again.

My mum came with me to get my MRI results. They showed me 3D scans so I was able to see the workings of my back, which was incredible. Then they broke the news that I had two worn discs in my lower back, four broken ribs and two fractured vertebrae, which meant it was really serious. They didn't know exactly what had caused my back problems and said it could have been down to genetics, trauma or simply bad luck. As my doctor had suspected, a lot of the scans showed evidence of old injuries. There was no other explanation for those other than my riding accidents.

I'd only just turned seventeen but I was told I had the back of someone three times my age. I'd learnt a bit about discs on my BTEC course so I kind of understood what they were, but I didn't know what it all meant for me in the long run.

The doctor said I had to have at least a year off from doing any kind of sport, and in particular, horse riding. Then he dropped the bombshell that if it didn't fully heal I might never be able to ride again. I remember that moment so clearly; I was absolutely devastated.

Riding had been my life since I was five years old and it still meant everything to me. I tried to be as upbeat about it as possible but I wanted to burst into tears there and then. I couldn't stop thinking about how different things would be. No more after college or weekend rides. That was what gave my days a structure and a purpose, and now it would all be taken away from me.

The hospital gave me loads of core exercises to do at home, and I also had to see a physio regularly to see if that helped. If it didn't the only option was for me to have an operation to put balloons in my back to stop it cracking any further (eek). The doctor said she'd try everything to stop that happening. Because I was young and still growing they wanted my body to have the opportunity to fix itself in a more holistic way before they did anything extreme. The main advice they gave me was 'don't have a big fall'. As least taking riding out of the equation meant there was a lot less risk of that.

The doctor was so sweet and said she didn't want to stop me living my life, but she did want to stop me injuring myself further. There was a danger if I had another really bad accident I could have been left permanently disabled. Her advice was 'if it hurts, don't do it'.

After the appointment Mum and Dad told me I absolutely had to stop riding. Crazily, a part of me thought that maybe I could still do it every now and again, mainly because I was so desperate to. But there was just no way. It was far too much of a risk. I also had to stop running, which was a real shame because that was something else I loved.

My parents kept a close eye on me because they didn't want me rushing into anything. They could tell when I was in pain because I would become really tired and my face would get very pale. I wasn't put on any medication, apart from paracetamol, because the doctors didn't want me to take strong drugs while I was so young. Instead I carried on as naturally as I could. As well as doing the core exercises, a local lady called Clare came to my house every week to give me a sports massage. While it didn't fix my back as such, it really helped with the aching and it meant my muscles were a lot more relaxed.

It was so hard not riding every day. Sometimes I'd wake up excited about taking Paddy out, and then it would hit me that I couldn't. I had several weeks of feeling down about the situation, but things were really put in perspective for me when my cousin, Maria, who was also seventeen, was diagnosed with lymph node cancer. It was such a shock because she was a really healthy, happy, lovely girl.

It was so horrible seeing Maria dealing with something so terrifying, and it really does make you reassess things. When she got the diagnosis her illness was already so advanced the doctors didn't know if she'd live beyond a week. The cancer had spread so much already and the only thing her family could do was pray she'd be OK.

Maria was in complete shock but instead of feeling sorry for herself she picked herself up, thought really positively and told herself she would be fine. When I saw how amazingly she was dealing with her illness it instantly made me snap out of any self-pity I was feeling. What I was going through seemed like such a big thing to me at first but there are people in much, much worse situations. It made me realise how fragile life can be.

Thankfully, after a lot of intense treatment, Maria recovered and she's in remission now. She's doing really well and she's still one of the happiest people I know. She follows her passions and she lives life on her own terms – I think because she feels lucky to be alive she makes the most of every day.

I'd still been having doubts about my BTEC course and when I realised I wouldn't be able to do any sport or go on to fulfil my goal of being a riding instructor it only reaffirmed what I was already feeling. It was pretty obvious that, taking everything into account, I had to leave college. I talked to my parents and they were amazing about it – they knew I hadn't been happy. Even though I had no idea what I was going on to next, they totally backed me.

I went into college on the Monday and spoke to

the deputy head. I told him I didn't want to continue with my course, and then for some reason I started crying. I think it was more relief than anything else. We talked everything through and he asked why I wanted to leave. I explained about my back but also said that I'd been unhappy for a while and this had been the catalyst for doing what felt like the right thing.

The deputy head told me he was sad because my grades had been good and he thought I could do really well if I stayed on. He asked if he could do anything to make me stay, but I had already made my mind up. I knew that I needed to make a fresh start, so maybe one good thing had come out of the awful situation with my back.

Ten minutes later I walked out of college and waved goodbye to my BTEC. Actually, leaving college was weird because clearly I didn't have what you'd call 'a plan'. It all happened so quickly. I didn't even have time to tell my friends I was leaving. I was going to phone them to let them know but I decided to give myself some time to get used to the idea so instead I told them I was taking some time off. Then the following week I broke the news that I wasn't going back at all.

They were all really shocked but they understood my reasons, although a couple of people predictably called me a dropout – everyone's got an opinion, and there had been lots of that throughout my life and I accepted it.

All I had to do now was work out my next move. I was college-free and career-free. What on earth was I going to do? I had to find out what else I was good at, but that can be much easier said than done. I decided to focus on getting my back better and wait for things to become a bit clearer. I carried on blogging about Alf and taking pictures and thankfully that kept me pretty busy.

Alf had just come into my life and if he hadn't been there as a focus things would have felt very different. I spent every afternoon with him and although I couldn't ride, I could still be around my horses and look after them, which was just as important. I didn't realise it then but Alfie came along at the perfect time. It was like he was a gift for me. He enabled me to stay positive even when things felt pretty rubbish.

Every morning I'd get up early and see to Badger,

Paddy and Pepper, and then I'd go and see Alf. Some days I'd spend from eight thirty until five thirty with him and our bond grew every day. I can't imagine what I would have done without him. I would have been very lost.

One day I was with Alfie when I realised I still really wanted to do a job where I could work with horses, so I started to explore possibilities beyond riding. A few days later I started a home study course on horse instincts and behaviour. The bulk of the work involved me studying horses, which was great because it justified me hanging out at the stables all the time!

At the end of February I decided the time had come for Alfie to become a gelding, which meant he was going to be castrated. I hated the idea of him having such a big operation but I knew it had to happen. He was already such a handful. Sometimes stallions can have a really nasty streak because their natural herd instincts kick in, which means they can be very protective. I noticed that as Alfie was getting older he was becoming increasingly protective over me and he wasn't always very nice towards other people. Sometimes he'd run towards them with his ears back, which is pretty aggressive. I didn't want that kind of behaviour to escalate so I was left with no choice.

It was the first time Alf was going to have an anaesthetic and because he was so small there was more of a risk. I'd read about instances where horses hadn't woken up from operations – the idea of losing Alf was too awful to think about and I had reason to be more nervous than most. We'd had an amazing German shepherd called Kim, who I adored, and when she was three she went in to be spayed. It's a really routine operation for a dog but I was still worried about her. I was fourteen at the time so I spent all day at school hoping she was OK.

When I got home that night I went straight to see Mum. I could see she was upset. She walked over and hugged me saying, 'Kim didn't make it.' I was so shocked I burst into tears. It was totally unexpected. Kim was so young and really healthy, but for some reason she hadn't come round from the anaesthetic.

I was so heartbroken and it took me ages to get over losing Kim. As a result I was petrified about the same thing happening to Alf. I phoned our vet, who had been with our family for several years, and had a long chat with him. He did his best to reassure me but I was still close to cancelling the operation. I kept getting tearful whenever I thought about it.

On the day of the operation I was beside myself. The vet arrived at Alf's stable and he could see I was in a state. 'He will be OK, won't he?' I said pleadingly. 'I don't know what I'd do without him.' He tried to calm me down by talking me through exactly what he was going to do, and then it was time.

Rather than sit outside his stable and panic, I decided the best thing to do was sit *in* there and panic. At least that way I could keep an eye on what was going on. I felt like if I was there when something went wrong I could somehow magically save Alf.

I was really conscious of how much sedation the vet was giving him and I asked a million questions so I was probably being a nightmare. As I've mentioned, I hate the sight of blood so that wasn't great either.

The procedure went really smoothly but when the vet asked me if I wanted to see what he'd done for some reason I said yes. I leant over to have a look at Alfie's wound and was nearly sick. It was so revolting. What was I thinking? Afterwards the vet showed me the bits he'd cut away and I was absolutely horrified. It wasn't the most fun afternoon I've had.

More importantly, Alf wasn't coming round very quickly after the operation, which was a massive concern. Horses should be awake and on their feet within half an hour but he wasn't stirring at all. I sat on the floor with his head between my knees stroking him. His eyes were rolled back in his head and his little tongue was hanging out. He looked so fragile.

As we edged towards the thirty-minute mark I started to feel very tense. Then suddenly Alf started to move his head a little bit and I felt like I could breathe normally again. My boy was going to be OK.

After the vet went I left Alf to sleep. He wasn't allowed any food or water for four hours because if he'd fallen asleep in his water bowl there was a risk he could have drowned. I went home for a few hours and then headed back to see him at eight p.m. As soon as I arrived he was whinnying his head off so I knew he feeling like himself again. I gave him some water and then went back home so he could get more rest.

Alf's undercarriage, as we'll call it, had to have eight weeks to heal after the operation. Because he's naturally really playful I had to make sure he didn't overexert himself. He wasn't allowed to run too much because he was still bleeding a lot, the poor thing.

The operation definitely changed Alf. He became a lot friendlier and less nibbly. When he was a stallion he wanted to be the dominant horse and he could be pretty boisterous, and he was also very keen on all female horses. That all calmed down after he had the snip and he's definitely a happier pony for it.

I've been really lucky because, apart from when he was gelded, Alf has never been really poorly or had to have any kind of operation. But if he's the slightest bit under the weather everything goes on hold and he acts like it's the end of the world. Even if he has a bit of a sniffle he stops eating and sighs a lot.

I'm used to Alf whinnying at me every time I approach his stable, but one morning when I went to give him his breakfast he didn't make a sound, which isn't like him at all. I started to panic in case something was wrong and all sorts of terrible things were going through my mind.

I ran over to his stable and when I got inside I realised that his food bucket was wrapped around his back left leg. There was a round bit of plastic attached to the side of the bucket and he'd somehow got his hoof through it. I have no idea how because the hole was smaller than the circumference of Alf's hoof. I guess it's a bit like when kids get their head stuck in railings or something.

I had to cut the plastic off his leg and he was being such a drama queen about it. He wasn't injured but he was walking around holding his leg up and hopping, totally milking it. I refused to pander to him and within ten minutes he was totally fine again. If you make a big deal of things so will Alf. But I've got wise to it.

A short while later I was trying to film him for an online clip and he wouldn't come over to me. My mum was standing with him and I said jokingly, 'Oh no, what's she done to you? Has Nanna upset you, Alf?' With that he wandered over and put his head on my leg as if something terrible had happened.

I left him in his field afterwards and he was screaming non-stop and hammering on the gate with his hooves. He was so loud our neighbours the Burtons came out to find what was going on. There was absolutely nothing wrong with him; he was just in a really clingy mood. I put him back in his stable and sat with him for a while and he was as happy as Larry after that. It is like having a child sometimes. He wants attention all the time.

*

Alf's got a little field shelter behind his fence and last summer, just after it had been built, I looked out of my bedroom window and I could see this little figure moving around behind it. He'd gone and squeezed himself into a tiny gap between his shelter and the fence. When you look at it you'd think there's no way he could fit in there so it must have taken some real effort.

I ran down and realised he was totally stuck. I tried to help him but it was impossible to wiggle him out. I went and fetched Mum and Dad and they had to help me push the fence back to try and free him. We were there for an hour trying everything we could think of, by which time Alf had fallen asleep because he was so exhausted by it all.

Dad said, 'I've got no choice but to get my tools and take down some of the fence.' Mum and I sat down waiting for Dad to come back from his shed when we heard a rustling sound. When we looked behind us Alf had managed to escape his wooden prison and he was happily running around his field.

He still goes behind there if he fancies a kip, it's become a little habit of his. But now if he gets 'stuck' I don't bother to try and rescue him because I know he'll come out when he wants to. He goes behind there most days at around two p.m. for a snooze and when people see him they say to me, 'Is your pony stuck?' and I'll reply, 'Nah, he's just really lazy.'

Sometimes Alf pretends he gets his head stuck in his fence too, which is done totally for effect. He'll poke his head through and then stare at me, willing me to go over and see him. He does it when I'm in my office a lot because he knows I can see him and he wants me to stop working and play with him. I feel really pressured because he won't take his eye off me but I can't give in because it will only encourage him.

Another time I was in my office working and he started pulling bits off his fence with his teeth and then looking at me. He knew I'd have to go down to see him and stop him. As well as ruining the fence it's dangerous because he could end up getting cut on any sharp bits, so I had no choice but to walk down the field to where he is. He totally knows what he's doing.

Sometimes Alf will do something mischievous, and then, as I get closer to him he'll stop doing it. He'll push plant pots over and by the time I've picked them back up again he'll be eating his food as if nothing has happened. I was once pushing a wheelbarrow full of muck and he kept trying to topple it over. Because I wouldn't let him he started pulling at the toggles of my wellies to get my attention. When that didn't work he started tugging at my jacket and making ridiculous growling noises.

One of his most annoying habits is pulling the toggles on jackets so the elastic stretches out really far. Then he lets them go again so they ping back and the pain when he catches you is awful. He does it to strangers too. I have to warn them to keep any toggles away from him.

I still talk to Alf all the time, like he's a human, and I'm sure he understands me. I'll ask him if he wants food or apple juice, which is one of his favourite treats, and he'll start jumping around when I do. It's not something I give him regularly because it's so sweet, but if I'm drinking some he'll put his face right up close to mine so I'll let him have the last little bit. I have to squeeze it out of the carton into my hand because he's not as clever as Paddy who can drink it through the straw. My horses do have some funny habits. I think their behaviour is a lot to do with how they're brought up and I've always treated mine like they're my equals rather than my pets. I'm pretty sure they think they're part human.

Ball Games

When I go away on holiday Alfie really sulks because he misses me. When I come back he gets so excited. Every year my dad and I go skiing somewhere and when I'm gone Alf misses me terribly. But skiing is one of the sports that I can still do so I can't bear to give it up – I count myself really lucky that I can still ski even though my back can be bad at times. Because I do a lot of running now and I've got a really strong core it means my back is more supported. Of course I still have to be really careful and I have had a couple of falls, which always worries me. But I pick myself up and carry on. As much as I don't want to push myself too much and end up injured again, I also don't want to be worrying all the time and I have to live my life.

The first time I went away Alf was not impressed. I'd never really left him at home before. My mum and brother aren't skiers so they stay behind, which meant Mum was on babysitting duty. Alf turned into a little terror that week. He kept trying to bite Mum on the bum whenever she went to feed him or let him out. He also darted off when she was holding his lead rope, and he went so fast she ended up face down in mud, and every time she tried to put him to bed he'd dodge her.

As soon as I got back he was an angel. He knew I was home because he knows my footsteps and when he saw me he was leaping around excitedly. For the next week he was following me around everywhere. I think he was scared I was going to leave again.

I won't lie; I miss Alf and my other pets loads when I travel. I've got camera systems set up so I can see Alf when I'm away, but I get emotional if we're apart for more than a week. I FaceTime and Skype my animals sometimes (I have to get someone to help out their end with that – they're not that clever), just to make sure they're OK. One time my brother FaceTimed me and Alf licked the screen of his iPhone so the whole thing was covered in slobber. John was not impressed.

If someone looks after Alf I'll leave a list of things they have to do that's as long as your arm. I find myself printing out sheets of A4 paper with strict rules on how everything has to be done. If someone who's never looked after the horses before is helping out we even have to have a dry run before I go so they know exactly what they're doing. I'm surprised anyone still offers, to be fair!

Luckily, even though he can be a nightmare, my family are always happy to help out with Alf and there's a lot of mutual love there. He and Dad love chasing each other around the fields and Alf definitely has a soft spot for him. They're like bros. If Alf was human they would go down to the pub together and talk about football.

Alf and my boyfriend Jonathan have become good mates now but it took a little while for Jonny to win him over. I met Jonny on New Year's Eve three years ago. He's the brother of one of my best friends and when he asked me out a couple of years ago things clicked into place. I wasn't looking for a boyfriend at the time but as if by magic he appeared.

Jonny came round for dinner one night a couple of months after we started seeing each other and was really nervous about meeting my parents. I said to him, 'You don't have to get past Mum and Dad but you do have to get past Alf. If Alf likes you we can be together, but it he doesn't it's not happening.'

A few months after we'd started seeing each other Jonathan offered to brush Alf for me while I was really busy. Even though Alf was getting used to Jonny by then he still wasn't convinced. He kept biting his feet and nudging him while he was trying to groom him. When Jonathan came back into the house he said, 'Your pony is being such a nightmare, he won't leave me alone!' He seemed quite scared and flustered – bearing in mind he's six feet two and in the army Alf must have really got to him.

Alf also has a habit of biting the feet of people he doesn't know. I have no idea why he does it but I need to try and train him out of it. Our postman came to chat to me the other day and Alf bent down (not that he has to bend very far, mind) and started biting his shoes. I was so embarrassed.

The good thing is Alf absolutely loves Jonathan now. I think it's because he's always feeding him Polos to win him over. I bought Jonny a drone for his birthday and Alf loves it. He likes chasing it when it flies past and they've really bonded over that.

Jonny knows that Alf is my priority and that I need regular time with him. Some boyfriends might think I'm a bit crazy but he really gets it. He doesn't even mind the fact that I have to phone home when we're out to make sure Alf's OK. I made it clear from day one that Alf and I come as a package.

I loved getting to spend my days with Alf while I worked on my home course, but I knew I had to start earning some money so I found a job working at an interior design shop in the next village along to me, Leyburn. I worked there five days a week as well as working at an Italian restaurant called Giovanni's three nights a week.

The interiors shop was called Quaint and Quirky and I had a lovely boss called Jeannette. It was a really small place and quite often I was the only person working there so I'd be stacking shelves, ordering products in, doing the books and serving customers. It was great experience because I got to do a bit of everything. The villages where I live are such a close-knit community so I knew a lot of the people who used to come into the shop – it was great for chatting to everyone and catching up on their news.

We also had a lot of tourists who visited so I became a bit of a tour guide. People would ask about the local area or the Dales in general. Leyburn is made up of drystone walls, barns and loads of hills, and I think people who live in cities find it incredibly old-fashioned. I was always getting asked why we had so many sheep and whether everyone who works around there is a farmer. Americans were always sur-prised by how much land there was and they were often confused about why all the fields haven't been built on. The answer is because it's farmland, and also because it's National Trust property, so no one is allowed to, thankfully.

Someone told me that until a few years earlier they'd thought the Dales were a made-up place which had been created especially for *Emmerdale*. They didn't realise that people really do live in places that remote. But I can assure you, it's very real.

To be fair, where I live does look like something out of *Emmerdale*. It's got a farm (of course!), a few shops and a pub. It's small and self-contained but I feel so lucky it's my home. Apart from the terrible countryside Wi-Fi signal.

When I look out of my bedroom window I can see hills for miles. On a clear day I can see right over to Middlesbrough. I'm surrounded by wildlife. Everywhere I look there are animals. It's mainly sheep, dairy cows and horses. We've also got a squirrel nest in our garden with about thirty adult and baby squirrels in it, and we get lots of birdwatchers wandering around because we've so many beautiful ones.

The Dales are full of woodland and proper country roads. Most of them are unmade and you can only fit one car down them so it can take quite a long time to get to places. They're mainly made up of gravel and a bit of tarmac but we don't have white lines down the middle or anything posh like that. They're very basic.

I don't think it's a big deal because I've always driven on bumpy roads. Some of the roads I use are just dirt tracks and they're not even featured on maps. It's not particularly Satnav friendly! Many of them haven't been treated for over twenty years so you wouldn't fare very well in a sports car, which is why everyone living here knocks about in beaten-up Land Rovers.

I'll often see free-range hens wandering around while I'm driving so I have to be really careful, and I'll see at least ten pheasants a day. There's a big river a mile outside of Leyburn so there are often lines of ducks walking along the road, and people are always riding horses through the villages.

I worked in Quaint and Quirky from nine a.m. until five p.m., and if I was due to work at night I'd head straight across the road to Giovanni's to do my waitressing stint. I'd be there from five thirty p.m. until ten p.m. and then go home, go to bed, get up early to spend time with the horses, and then go to work again.

It was an amazing way to build up some savings but it meant I didn't have a lot of time to spend with my animals, so I decided to start doing half days at the interiors shop. I'd go home in the afternoon and spend time with the horses, and then head back into town in the evening, pop on my pinny and serve customers pizzas and wine.

My boss at Giovanni's was also great. She was called Claire and was always so nice to me, even when I made the odd mistake. Being so clumsy definitely meant there were more than a few . . . One day I was carrying a tray of drinks over to a family and the dad had ordered a pint of beer. Just as I was putting the drinks on the table the pint tipped over and soaked their four-year-old little boy. They smiled and said, 'Ah well, at least he's had his first drink now!' His parents laughed it off but I was mortified.

I also burnt myself several times and dropped a few meals here and there. One time a huge plate of spaghetti Bolognese slipped out of my hand and the plate *bounced* on the floor, sending the food flying everywhere. I also smashed a fair few glasses. Claire was very understanding, and even though I'd offer to pay for any breakages she always refused to take the money out of my wages.

While I was keeping on top of all my various jobs, courses and responsibilities towards looking after all my animals, Alf's blog was really taking off. I had over three thousand followers, which was so exciting, but it also meant that he was becoming better known. Word spread around the local area and Alf started getting a lot of visitors. I'd arrive at the yard at weekends and there would be people there wanting to meet him. Sometimes I'd turn round while we were in the field and there would be someone randomly snapping a photo of him. I also started getting Facebook messages from people I didn't know asking if they could come and meet him. I was walking Alf down the road one day when a car pulled up and a woman leaned out and said, 'Is that Little Alf? My kids love him.'

As brilliant as it was that everyone seemed to love Alf, it also made me nervous. It suddenly hit me that if someone wanted to steal him they wouldn't have a hard time finding him. The yard had CCTV and I spoke to Diane who promised to keep an eye out for me. Of course the other horses were at just as much risk of being stolen as Alf, but the difference was that Alf would easily fit in the back of someone's car, whereas someone trying to run off with a full-size horse would attract a bit more attention.

Alf and I would play for hours and every time

I gave him a new toy he got so excited. One day I put a football into his field with him and he started nudging it with his nose and chasing it around. He was having the time of his life and when I decided to try and teach him to fetch it and roll it he picked it up in no time. He seemed to really enjoy showing off his new skills so I started teaching him more tricks.

At first I tried a method called Natural Horsemanship. It's a bonding technique which is very gentle. It's all to do with dominance and instincts. It didn't really work with Alf because I think he found it a bit boring, so I moved to clicker training. I was already doing clicker trainer with my German Shepherd, Sasha, and we'd been to some classes, so I knew how well it worked, but it's not a very standard way to teach horses. I'd heard about people being really successful using it on horses in America before so I didn't think it would hurt to try. Alf is basically like a dog anyway and he responded really well to it. He was often around Sasha while I was training her because we'd all go for walks together sometimes, so he picked up similar habits to her. I'm pretty sure for a while he thought he was a German Shepherd too. To be fair they are pretty much the same height.

The first thing I taught Alf was 'kiss'. He naturally

puts his head up to me all the time anyway so I developed that into a 'kiss' trick by kissing his nose, clicking and then giving him a treat. Now every time I say 'kiss' he'll raise his nose ready for me and it's so cute.

Most of the time I don't even have to ask, as soon as I walk over to him he's got his nose in the air waiting for one. His little eyes will be looking up at me and if I don't kiss him straight away he starts nudging me. If he wants another kiss, sometimes he'll chase me round until I give in.

He doesn't kiss anyone else apart from me. Sometimes he'll deceive people into thinking he's going to give them a kiss so they'll bend down then he'll nip them, which is really bad. He puts his nose up to my mum sometimes and when she bends down he'll put his top lip up and try to nip her chin. You'd think she'd know not to do it by now but she's always hopeful he'll change his ways!

The next thing I tried was to get Alf's basket out and try and teach him to close the lid. Every time he did it I'd press my training clicker, treat him and pet him.

I talked to him all the time to try and teach him new words. I'd often get caught out by people while

I was having proper conversations with Alf at the yard. One day I was telling Alf all about a book I was reading when a local friend popped her head about the stable door and said, 'Who are you talking to?' I looked a bit embarrassed and when she realised I was talking to Alf she started laughing and said, 'You carry on. I don't care what anyone says I think it's good for horses to have a proper education!'

Oh dear.

Chapter 5

Many Trick Pony

I worked out early on that Alf doesn't have a great attention span so I only do quick ten-minute training sessions with him. Little and often seems to work best. His favourite toy is a special horse ball that he whacks around with his nose. Sometimes he's a bit vicious with it and it's quite painful if it hits you! It's got loads of teeth marks in it, and he loves it because he knows if he does a trick he's going to get a treat.

I got Alf a big wooden block and I taught him to stand on it. Now every time he goes into his paddock he runs and stands on it really proudly and waits for his treat as if he's performing for an audience.

I also bought him a big yoga ball because I thought it was something that would be hard for him to pop. But ... no. He popped it within a day and when I picked up the sad, crumpled mess I saw that it had one of his baby teeth stuck in it. It was only the size of my little nail. Considering how massive Alf's head is his baby teeth are stupidly small.

I got Alf a replacement yoga ball and before he was gelded he used to get a bit frisky with it. A friend's kids came to visit him one day just as he was showing it a good time in his paddock. All the children started saying, 'What's he doing?' and I had to run over and take the ball off him as quickly as I could.

Alf still loves playing with that giant ball now and he rolls over it as if he's actually doing yoga. I might try and teach him some moves at some point. He already does quite a good downward dog, but I can imagine he'll be great at the mountain pose. I have no idea why he hasn't popped this one yet, but I wonder if it's because it's blue and his other ones were red. Seriously! I think he may prefer the colour. I know it sounds ridiculous but he definitely likes this one more.

Alf is also a big fan of yoghurt pots because he likes the smell, and he really loves teddy bears. He's got his own 'Alf' teddy, which he's very keen on. I'm not sure if he knows that it's him or not but he definitely likes it more than his other teddies.

One thing Alf hates is garden ornaments. He's always breaking them so I have to keep him away from them. We used to have a giant sheep ornament and I think he was probably jealous of it because it was nearly the same size as him. We were walking past it one day and he pulled me over to it and then kicked it, smashing it into hundreds of pieces.

We've got ornaments on the front step going up to our house and when I was taking him for a walk one day we passed my mum. He really wanted her to stroke him so he went over and started nudging her, but she was carrying some logs so she couldn't. He got really cross so he ran over to the steps and knocked all the ornaments flying, much to Mum's dismay.

I bought Alf a padding pool last summer, which wasn't the best idea considering he's not a huge fan of water, but my dogs got some use out of it. That was until Alf stood in it when it didn't have any water in it and he seemed to quite like it, but within a matter of days he'd nibbled one of the sides and it swiftly deflated.

I've taught Alf some new tricks recently so now he can pick things up, put them in his basket, close the lid, and then lift it back up and take things out again. He won't do anything unless it's me who asks him to. Other people have tried to get him to do stuff and he just walks off. It's weird how animals will only interact with certain people. Horses love their owners and they're very loyal so they tend to stick with one person. Alf thinks I'm his mum and he wants to be with me as much as possible. If for some reason I'm late to see him in the morning he'll start shouting for me. I can hear him from inside the house and I have to go or he won't shut up.

He's so spoilt I even have to make sure I use the 'right' sized balls when we're training because he finds ones that are too big a bit intimidating so he refuses to play with them. That's how bad things have got. Everything he owns is small – Alf sized – even his brush and lead rope. I find his things online or have them specially made. His training steps are handmade, believe it or not, shops don't stock min-iature flights of stairs for tiny horses . . .

Alf can squeak things now, including a horn.

It's so funny because it sounds like he's talking. Imagine if that was actually Alf's voice? If I put it on a step he'll squeak it and then look around to see who's giving him attention. Sometimes he'll get scared of the noise too. I don't know how he doesn't expect it to be so loud when he does it so often, but he'll look really shocked as if to say, 'how did that happen?'

He can also open the door to his stable. I've also got him some skittles for the garden so he rolls a ball and knocks those over. Or if he's feeling naughty he'll run up and kick them over with his tiny feet.

He's got a bubble blower and he loves chasing bubbles around the paddock, but I don't think he really understands why they disappear so quickly. When the mood takes him he can jump through a hoop, although he's not terribly keen and it takes a lot of bribing to make him to do it. I have to be armed with treats if I want to lure him through, and even then he'll demand payment upfront.

Someone in America taught their horse to paint so I've been working on that. As soon as he's mastered it I can send him out to decorate people's houses so he can earn his keep.

I get asked by a lot of people how they can train

their own horses so I put tutorials up on YouTube, but I make it clear I'm not a trained professional. I don't know everything about horses and there are lots of people who know a lot more than me. Often when people think about training they see it as teaching a pet to be obedient, or being a dominant leader. Personally, I don't see it that way at all. For me, training it about creating a bond, trust, understanding and a lasting friendship. It's a great way of communication and learning all about your pet, and it doesn't have to involve you shouting at them, or trying to get them to do everything you say. I don't ever use force or negative methods, and I've managed to teach my animals to do all sorts of things using love and patience, so I'm proof that it works.

Once your pet trusts and cares for you they'll want to work with you. It makes sense, doesn't it? Animals can be very like children, and often if you force children into doing things they either sulk or rebel – animals are the same. You'll get a lot further with a happy horse than you will with a stressed out, put-upon one.

If I were to give my top five tips for training they would be:

1. Be patient, because it does take time. I've been to training events and I've seen people getting cross with their animals because they're not doing what they want, but they're not always going to get things overnight.

2. Listen to them. You can usually tell if they don't want to do something so there's no point in forcing them.

3. Give them a reward to let them know they've done well.

4. Make it fun. Training should be enjoyable for them. They're just like humans. They find it easier to learn things when they're having fun.

5. End on a good note. Even if they haven't done what you want them to or they've been really naughty, give them a treat at the end of training because otherwise they'll have a negative view of training in general.

People love seeing Alf doing his tricks, but they also love the videos where he's being naughty. I put up a video of him sneaking into the house and the response from Alf's followers was brilliant. Any videos of him running around go down well, probably because he looks pretty ridiculous.

Anything where Alf and I are interacting is popular too. When I get Mum to film videos of us they get loads of views. It's funny because when I started to include myself in photos and videos along with Alf we got more followers. I think it's because people can see how close we are. I realised that hashtags are really important and help to get the right people following you, so use them a lot. In fact, #iprobablyhashtagtoomuch

Alf was made for social media. As soon as he sees the camera he starts acting differently. He'll mess about and show off. He's picked up the video camera in his teeth before, and he's also knocked it over numerous times. He licks it and rubs his bum against it, which doesn't make the filming process particularly easy.

I sometimes have to get close up to Alf to shoot the videos and if I'm wearing a beanie hat he'll try and snatch it off my head. I like leaving bloopers on videos so people can see them, but I've had to edit a few out because they look quite vicious. I know Alfie would never hurt me though. He would be beside himself if he did.

Alf's got fans all over the world now, which is crazy. And although loads of his fans are quite young, he's got lots of older ones too. Quite often at events parents will encourage their kids to come over and get a photo with him and it's so obvious it's because they want one but they're too embarrassed to ask.

The comment I get most on social media about Alf is 'Awww, he's cute!' Or 'he looks naughty'. If I say he's having his flu jab or something, people will message asking how he is, which is so sweet. I get the odd unkind comment about his dwarfism and I have to resist the urge to jump in and defend him because it would probably just encourage people. In my eyes (and his) he's perfect, and that's all that matters.

I get a lot of likes when I dress Alf up. He's got his own dressing-up box that keeps on growing. He's got bunny ears for Easter, Pudsey ears for Children in Need day, and horns and a cape for Halloween. He genuinely likes it when the box comes out because he knows it means I'm going to take photos of him.

He's a proper poseur, so much so that he loves looking at himself in mirrors or glass. We've got two big windows on the outside of my mum's painting cabin and he stands in front of them checking himself out. He'll tilt his head or shake it from side to side and gaze at his reflection. He likes looking at himself in puddles too. I should really get him a big mirror for his stable. I don't think he'd ever get bored of looking at himself.

He also likes dressing up on his birthday so I've got him a little birthday hat. He was born on April Fools' Day (I know!) and every year I make sure he knows it's his special day. Well, three days, because I stretch his birthday out for as long as possible. In my family we always have a birthday eve the night before, then the actual birthday, and then a birthday Boxing Day. Any excuse to make a fuss of Alf: last year I made him a horse cake out of carrots and molasses. It was only a small one but he loved it. I also put up banners and spoiled him rotten with presents. I got him a new lick, a ball, a collar – all sorts. He'll generally eat everything he can first and then move on to the toys. Alf has his priorities right.

He loves all the dogs' toys as well so he's always trying to nick them. But if anyone tries to take *his* then there's trouble. I keep all his toys in the paddock and if Pepper goes in there, Alfie gets really protective and starts warning him off. I have to take them all out so it doesn't cause problems. As well as playing with toys Alf loves trainers and shoes.

Thankfully the dogs are really understanding. I think they're aware that Alf has got delusions of grandeur so it's not worth challenging him. The dogs get on pretty well with Alf and he and Sasha play football together sometimes, but she can get a bit excited and start jumping up and barking. That's when Alf gets scared and runs away so I find myself chasing him around the field again. Sasha also grabs the football in her mouth and runs away with it, which I think Alf probably finds a bit annoying.

Most of my animals are friends. I should probably introduce you to them all. Though Alf thinks it's all about him, there are so many other four-legged friends in the family . . .

Sasha and Maggie, my cocker spaniel, are really close. Maggie barks a lot but she's adorable. My nanna and grandad have got her sister, Molly, and they love spending time with each other. I remember going with my parents and John to pick Maggie up when I was nine and John was ten. She was still a puppy and she was so tiny. On the drive home we pulled into McDonald's. Maggie woke up at that exact moment and John and I sneakily fed her a chip. That's my earliest memory of her and even now McDonald's reminds me of that day.

Maggie was the runt of the litter so she was always going to have a few problems and need more care than other dogs. She had lumps on her body that she had to have removed, and she had to have a few operations for various health issues. She's always needed a lot of TLC. Because of that she's always been the baby of the family, even though at eleven she's one of the oldest animals.

Though Maggie is blind now she's still such a happy girl. She knows her way around the house instinctively and she knows where everything should be. If I leave my riding boots out or someone moves a plant pot there's a good chance she'll bump into them so we have to be really careful.

Sasha takes good care of her and Maggie often follows her around. Sasha will keep stopping to make sure she's OK, it's adorable how Sasha looks after her. We always know if something isn't right with Maggie because Sasha will moan on her behalf, and then one of us will go over and see what's wrong with her. To be fair, it's usually because she wants a treat. She and Alf have that in common.

We got Sasha about two months after we lost Kim, and she's five now. She's gorgeous and really funny and she always tries to sit on your lap even though she's massive. It's weird because Sasha does some of the same things Kim used to do, like nicking your crisps when you're not looking. Kim used to be mad about prawn crackers and Sasha is exactly the same. If ever we get a Chinese takeaway we have to keep a sharp eye on them or she'd have the lot.

Because of what happened with Kim we're too nervous to send Sasha to be spayed so she won't ever be. I wouldn't be able to handle it if anything happened to her. People underestimate how much you grow to love your pets. They really do become a part of the family and sometimes you spend more time with them than you do your actual family. I'm closer to my pets than I am to some of my cousins. I see my pets every day, whereas I see some of my cousins about three times a year.

When you have pets from when they are tiny babies you feel such a responsibility towards them. I see my animals as friends. I really do. My mates will ask what I'm doing that day and I'll say, 'I'm just messing about with the boys.' I'm talking about the horses, which they find odd. If I'm ever bothered about something or I've got a problem I'll spend an hour with the horses and I'll feel better. When I've gone through hard times they've made everything so much better. I'll sit with my lop-eared rabbit, Malibu, in the morning if things are playing on my mind and just by taking the time out with her I feel so much calmer. It's like a form of therapy.

Sasha is such a softie and she's even calm around my rabbits and guinea pigs. She'll go up to their hutches and sniff them and paw at the door. Sometimes Malibu will put his feet up so their paws touch and it's so cute. People always say you shouldn't put rabbits and guinea pigs together but mine live in the same hutches and they get on really well. In fact, if I separate them they pine for each other and stop eating.

The girls and the boys have to be kept apart though, because otherwise I'd have loads of babies. I did think about getting Malibu neutered but there's only a fifty-fifty chance he'd survive. Because of their size, sedation can be pretty dangerous for small animals, and for some reason it's even worse for rabbits. After what happened to Kim I could never take that risk.

Malibu lives with Hamish, my male guinea pig, live together during the day and then have their own sleeping quarters at night. And then Holly, Candy and Muffles, the female guinea pigs and rabbit, are together full time because they love spending time with each other. Muffles is a white Lionhead rabbit who has one blue eye and one brown eye and looks a bit like an alien. Holly sits on Muffles' head and grooms her, so Holly has always got loads of fluff in her mouth.

They all live in a big heated barn with glass windows and fake grass and they love it, but that doesn't stop them coming into my office with me when I'm working sometimes. They're good company.

Their living area is like a hotel with the boys on the bottom and the girls on the top. The boys have big beds and tubes and tunnels for them to run through. The girls have a luxury apartment up the top with a big run and a really comfy bedroom with big dog beds in so they've got somewhere lovely to sleep. They even have fans to keep them cool in the summer and they like stretching out in front of them. It's so funny because you can see their fur gently blowing up and down in the wind. It's only a matter of time before I build them a little spa.

I buy them fancy spinach sometimes and they think all their Christmases have come at once. It's so expensive I wouldn't even buy it for myself but I seem to think it's fine to get it for them! They are very pampered.

Twinkle, my Robo dwarf hamster, lives on his own, although he does have a Little Alf teddy to keep him company. He's really intrigued by the real Alfie whenever he comes into the house. Robos are incredibly cute and Twinkle is so intelligent. He knows when it's feeding time and when his water's being topped up, and when I walk over to the cage he runs to the door because he wants me to take him out. He's so small I have to be really careful when I handle him, but he's gorgeous.

Alf met Twinkle recently and they got on really well. *Sort* of. I was cleaning Twinkle's cage out in our kitchen (my mum was not impressed) and I put Twinkle in his little plastic ball so he could run around. Then I decided to take Twinkle to see Alf, so I carried him down to his stable and I let Alf have a little sniff of him through the air holes. They were really intrigued with each other, and when I put Twinkle on the floor Alf started rolling his ball with his nose and licking the plastic. Twinkle wasn't in the least bit fazed, and I twigged afterwards that Alfie probably thought his plastic runaround was a football.

Obviously I didn't leave them alone together or anything and I made sure Alf didn't roll the ball too fast, but they've met a couple of times since and they've become firm friends.

It's actually got a bit out of hand and I've now got more pets than ever. There are twelve of them at the moment, which sounds like quite a lot. Having said that, I'd definitely have more if I could but I have to be a little bit sensible. I've always wanted a snake and a hawk. I used to work at Thorp Perrow, which is a big bird of prey and mammal centre near me, and being around the incredible birds meant there was a time when I was seriously considering getting a hawk. But farmers have been known to shoot birds of prey and I didn't want to put one in danger.

My animals are a bit of a funny combination but somehow it works. Alf and Pepper are really good friends, but Badger and Paddy still don't really get on with Alfie. Obviously they got off to a bad start and I think they're quite jealous of him. Even though I make sure I share my affection equally, in their eyes he still gets special treatment. I would never put Alf into a field with Badger and Paddy because I wouldn't trust them with him. They're very instinctive and they know when another horse is vulnerable.

In September 2016 I popped out to the shop and

left Alf in his paddock. When I got back home I could hear some noise, but because the horses often make a racket I didn't think too much of it. When it carried on I walked down to see what was happening and when I looked into Alfie's paddock he wasn't there. This really horrible feeling came over me and when I heard a sound that was like a cross between a whinny and a cry I knew straight away it was Alf. I've never heard a sound like that come out of him before, and I never, ever want to again.

I dashed down to the field where the noise was coming from and I saw that Badger and Paddy had Alf on the floor and they were attacking him. I was so scared. They were kicking and biting him and he couldn't get up. It was like a group of older boys bullying a younger kid in the playground and it was so sad to see.

I had no choice but to run into the field and try and fight them off. I climbed over the fence and belted over to the group of them. I didn't even think about the fact I was putting myself in danger because my protective instinct kicked in. I was crying my eyes out and Badger backed away, but I had to pull at Paddy's mane to try and get him off Alf.

As soon as Alf had some space around him he took

his chance and got up, swished his tail at Badger and Paddy and walked off. He was putting on a front but I could tell he was scared. It was so upsetting to think of the damage Pepper and Badger could have caused him if I hadn't got to him when I did. He's got a delicate back because of his size and condition so they could have done irreparable damage. If we're talking worst case scenario, they could have killed him.

I got Alf's head collar on and led him back into his stable. I sat with him until he felt better but he wasn't himself at all. He was standing with his little head down, feeling really sorry for himself.

I didn't go and see Badger and Paddy for the rest of the day because I was so angry with them, but when I went down that evening neither of them would look at me. They knew what they'd done was very wrong, and I think it's safe to say Alf won't be breaking into their field again any time soon.

Pepper and Alfie get up to all sorts together and they really wind each other up, they're a very funny pair. They always bite each other's ankles, and you can guarantee if one of them is doing something they shouldn't be, the other one will start doing it too. Pepper is thirty-four inches so he's eight inches taller than Alfie, but it's Alf who rules.

It's funny because Alf and Pepper were the ones who hated each other most to start with. Pepper would pin his ears back and show signs of aggression towards Alf, and he wouldn't accept him into the herd. Somehow, along the way they became best friends and now they absolutely worship each other. It took a few months but now they groom each other and run around together very happily.

Pepper is fourteen years old now so sometimes he likes his peace. Sadly for Pepper, Alf doesn't always give it to him, so if he's being annoying I'll move one of them into a separate field so Pepper gets some time to himself. Though Pepper does get his own back – sometimes when they're messing around Pepper will push Alf over and if Alf's feeling lazy he can't be bothered to get up so he lies there pretending he's been hurt. I'll have to go out and help him back onto his tiny feet and miraculously he starts to feel better.

Pepper used to be so well behaved and quiet and sweet, but the moment he met Alf that all changed. They gang up together like Power Rangers and chase me round the paddock. That can be funny, but it wasn't the time I was carrying two large buckets of water and they knocked me over. I got completely drenched.

Alf when he first arrived and was even littler! Who could have guessed the adventures we'd have?

My early days of horse riding, before I was injured, here with Badger

In the ménage with Star on one of my first ever riding lessons

Alf with all his friends: Badger, Paddy and Pepper

Some other animal buddies!
Below with Alfie and Sasha

Muffles

Twinkle, the
hamster

Malibu the rabbit, with
his favourite toy . . .

Candy, Floss and
Holly, the guinea pigs

Time for a kickaround – Alf makes a great striker

All the fun training with Alf

I don't think I'm going to get that shoe back . . .

Time for a
tea break!

Alf with his
crow friend

Who doesn't
like being
spoilt on their
birthday?

#HAPPY
BIRTHDAY
♥ALF♥

Alfie with the Brooke Charity in Bolesworth

Being interviewed at the Great Yorkshire Show

Outside the new Little Alf shop!

One of our most exciting days,
meeting Princess Anne

Nothing beats life at home
with Little Alf

They've even escaped together a few times, which is such a nightmare. When they were at the old yard they managed to break through a fence and ran off into the woods together so I had to go searching for them. They also managed to get the gate of their field open at the house we're in now and I was chasing them around for about an hour. I was shaking a bucket of pony nuts to try and lure them over but because they were together they were standing firm. They knew it was much harder to get them both back inside and they played on it.

The thing is, Alf is too clever now. I've trained him to do things too well so he can open gates if they're not completely secure. We have to buckle them, and then also tie them up because he can undo the buckles.

The worst thing Pepper and Alf ever did together was attack my dad's orchard. I'd had a really busy day sorting things out in my office so I hadn't had a chance to do my midday check on them. At around three thirty it looked like it was going to rain so I decided to bring them in for the night. I put Badger and Paddy in their stables but when I went to get Pepper and Alfie they weren't in their paddock and the gate was wide open.

I knew they couldn't be too far away because our

land has got fencing all around it, but after searching all the fields they were nowhere to be found. I started to get really worried. I was about to phone my mum in a panic when I heard Alfie whinnying. I followed the noise and found the pair of them in my dad's orchard. Pepper was standing in my dad's beloved water fountain having a lovely time, while Alf was helping himself to apples from a little tree, the thief.

Pepper isn't the only horse Alf rules over. In fact, it appears Alf thinks he rules the equine world. Recently a Sussex Punch called Mango moved into the field next door to Alf. They're the biggest horses in the horse kingdom, but he'd barely had a chance to settle in before Alfie started terrorising him. Punches are known to be nice natured and Alfie obviously decided to take advantage.

Instantly Alf was like, 'what are you doing on my turf?' and started whinnying at him. Then he started cantering up and down by the fence to try and scare him, and then he stuck his head through the fence to try to bite poor Mango's knees.

Mango is almost two and half times the size of Alf, but it's clear who's in charge. No horse is safe when Alf's around.

Alf also flirts with another horse called Millie who is at least twice his size. He genuinely thinks he's in with a chance, and whenever she's around he'll show off by swishing his head around and taking really dainty steps. It's so funny.

When I look at all the animals I own, it's pretty obvious that I'm drawn to ones that have problems. I always end up with creatures that need a lot of care.

Alf's got his dwarfism, an overshot jaw, and a wonky left leg. His knees are also a little higher than they should be but that doesn't affect him. It just makes his trot a bit different to other horses. Poor Paddy was mistreated and set on fire so he's very nervous. He's also got some growth problems so his front end is smaller than his back end. Pepper's got sweet itch, Badger's got arthritis and funny feet, Maggie's blind and Sasha's missing quite a few teeth. My guinea pig, Floss, who died recently, had webbed feet, and Malibu can't hop because he's got a dodgy foot. Muffles has attachment issues so if I go away on holiday she stops eating. Hamish and Holly are brother and sister and both are really tiny and haven't grown like they should. Twinkle is fine. I rescued him last Christmas because he shared a cage with his siblings and they kept giving him a hard time. But apart from being bullied he's in pretty good shape.

All in all they're a bit of a motley crew but I wouldn't change a single one of them. They make me smile each day and one thing's for sure, I'm never bored!

Chapter 6

Annoying the Neighbours

I've always loved writing short stories and because Alf was such a character I came up with the idea of writing a book about his adventures. Even if it was just for me it felt like a really nice, fun thing to do. At that stage I wasn't planning to release it or anything, but I missed writing and Alf was great inspiration.

Sometimes in the evenings I'd have a bit of spare time so one night I sat down and started writing. I didn't have much of a plan but I knew I wanted the story to include some kind of magic.

I wrote whatever came to mind and it seemed to

just flow. I didn't stop and analyse anything or worry about how it sounded because it was only for me, and maybe my family, to enjoy. It was so nice not to be concerned about what other people would think.

I had no clue how long a kids' book should be so I followed my instincts and wrote until it felt like the story came to a natural end. I called it *The Magical Adventure of Little Alf: The Discovery of the Wild Pony* and was really pleased with it. Once it was completed I reread it several times and thought that maybe I could put it out there for other people to enjoy after all. It certainly wouldn't hurt to try.

I didn't have a clue how to go about getting a book published but I knew of a local author, a very nice man called Donald, so I contacted him to ask him for some advice. He suggested that I took a look at a website called Lulu, which is a self-publishing company that enables you to print your own book.

I had a look around the site and it appeared to be surprisingly straightforward. What did I have to lose? Nothing ventured nothing gained and all that. I set up an account, designed the cover myself using a photo of Alf, added some illustrations I'd drawn for the inside pages, and then I ordered my very first copy of my very first book.

I hadn't told my parents what I was up to and when it landed on the doorstep my mum said, 'What on earth is this?' They couldn't believe I'd written a book about Alfie. It was only a sample copy but the feeling I got when I held that book in my hand was . . . I was just so proud.

I took it to the stables the following day and sat eating sweets and reading it to Alf. It's fair to say he wasn't my most appreciative audience because just as I was getting to the climax of the story he drifted off to sleep. There's gratitude for you! I read it to him a few times afterwards and he'd nuzzle it or put his hooves up while I sat with him, so now it's smeared with mud and nose marks. Typical.

It was crazy to think that I'd created a complete book. It looked really professional and impressive. But then I realised I had some serious work to do if I ever wanted it to be stocked in shops. The front cover didn't look right because the photo wasn't great quality once it was blown up, and I'd used the wrong font so it looked more like a business manual than a kids' book. Then when I read through the text I spotted loads of spelling mistakes. I was horrified.

I did all the necessary corrections and then I

ordered another copy, which also turned out to have quite a few mistakes in it. Oops.

I'm not one to give up easily so made the additional corrections, ordered another book and – you guessed it – there were more mistakes. In the end it took me six attempts to get it right, but it was all worth it. I was beyond happy with the finished product.

In May 2014 it was all change for my family because we moved into a new house in Finghall. I was ecstatic because it meant we had our own land and stables, so all the horses could come and live with us.

When we first moved, the stables weren't quite finished, so all my horses were still in their old homes. I could only see Alf for a short time each day because our new place was quite far away from Diane's yard and I still didn't drive at that time, so I relied on lifts from people. I missed Alf so much that in the end Dad offered to build him a temporary stable, which was so tiny and cute. And, thankfully, escape proof.

When the other horses arrived they hadn't seen Alf for several months, and because he was already there when they moved in they were coming onto his territory, rather than the other way round. It already smelt of him and the grass was low from where he'd eaten it, and that meant he had the upper hand so they were a lot more accepting towards him.

All the horses had their own individual stables and I was able to see them from my bedroom window. Dad set up CCTV so I could also watch them inside their stables. It was much more secure for the animals, which meant I didn't have to worry about Alf getting stolen anymore.

People always say Alf's got the best stable because he's my favourite, but he hasn't, honestly. His stable isn't posher than any of the other horses but it has got special matting on the walls so he doesn't bang his head on the breeze block. We recently got it for Pepper because they're both at a different level to the other horses, so it would be easier for them to bang their heads or rub themselves and get scabs.

He's also got the brightest stable with the most windows because he spends the most time inside. He loves spending time in his stable and he likes being snug. He's got a rug that goes over him when it's cold and he's even got his own beanie hat that he wears sometimes. It's a little red one with ear holes cut out of it. He's also got a blue scarf with sheep on, and I'll often wrap one my own hoodies around his neck as well because he likes the fact it smells of me.

His stable is also nearest to the tack room because I can let him out in the morning and he'll follow me around and do my duties with me. He comes into the tack room to get everything ready, and then he's by my side while I feed the other horses.

We'd been in the new house for a matter of days before Alf started causing trouble with the neighbours. I still cringe when I think about it now.

I'd gone out for the day and my dad had said he'd look after Alf. When it started raining Dad went to put Alf back in his stable, because of course it would have been a disaster if he'd got wet. Mainly because he hates it (I do wonder if he's scared he's going to shrink!), but also because it can affect his muscles and make it a bit painful for him to walk, in the same way people's muscles can get sore if they get wet and cold.

Dad was trying to get Alf's head collar on but he was being really badly behaved and he kept moving his head around so Dad couldn't loop it over. Then when Alf noticed that my dad had left the gate to the field open he dashed towards it, zoomed through and went running off into the distance. Dad chased after him but, as I've said, even though Alf is tiny he's pretty speedy so there was no way he could catch up.

Our new house was still a bit of a building site and there were no fences up anywhere, and Alf ran straight past all the builders into next door's garden. Dad found him twenty minutes later in Mr and Mrs Burton's vegetable patch having a proper feast. That garden is their pride and joy and he'd bitten through all their expensive netting and he was gobbling up their Brussels sprouts, lettuces and tomatoes. Dad said Alf looked like he was having the time of his life, and all he could do was stand there horrified, wondering how on earth he was going to sort out the mess.

We were probably already in the Burtons' bad books because of all the noisy building work that was going on right under their nose, and then Alf wolfed down all of the veg they'd been lovingly growing. So much for making a good impression.

Dad went and knocked on the door, ready to deliver a very big apology, but the Burtons were out so he decided the best thing to do was just get Alf home and then pop back later to explain everything.

Dad managed to get Alf back into his stable but by the time I got home he'd gone out so I didn't see him. I was having a cup of tea in front of the TV when there was a knock on the door. When I opened it Mrs Burton was standing there looking a bit upset.

'We think your horse has rummaged through our vegetable patch,' she said. 'Everything's been dug up and it's full of small hoof prints.'

I immediately thought there was no way Alf would have done that. I mean, it *sounded* like the kind of thing he would do, but he'd definitely been in his field stable all day. Hadn't he?

'I'm really sorry,' I said. 'But it couldn't have been Alf. He's been here all the time. My dad's been looking after him for me. I hope you find out who did it, but it definitely wasn't Alf.'

Mrs Burton clearly didn't believe me and as she left I started to wonder whether Alf was capable of getting himself in and out of his field without anyone noticing?

When Dad got home I told him about Mrs Burton accusing Alf of making a mess of her vegetable patch. As I sighed and did my third exasperated head shake Dad looked very awkward and said, 'Hannah, there's something I need to tell you.'

Dad told me the story and it took all my courage to walk down the road and knock on the Burtons' door ready to make the biggest apology of my life. I could feel my heart beating really fast and my hands felt hot and sticky as I rang the doorbell. When Mrs Burton answered I smiled as sweetly as I could and explained that, yes, my badly behaved pony had guzzled all her prized vegetables and I was very, very, very sorry. I must have said sorry about fifty times.

Thankfully Mrs Burton was very understanding. I think she realised that I genuinely hadn't known anything about Alf's escape. I promised her we'd try not to let Alf near their garden again, and I even offered to do some gardening for her to make up for it.

We get on really well with the neighbours and they're such nice people, but even now I still apologise when I see them. They've got to know Alf since 'the' incident and they think he's lovely, but I'm still mortified.

Not surprisingly, because he was full of the Burtons' lettuces and tomatoes, Alf didn't need much dinner that night. But as I looked at him I thought back to the very early days when it was hard to get him to eat anything apart from grass. It took me two years just to teach him to eat Polo mints because he was so wary of them, but now he can't get enough.

In fact, food and sleeping are two of his favourite things. His current favourite foods are carrots, apples and marshmallows, even though they're bad for him. He also loves the herbs in my parents' herb garden and he munches on them anytime he gets a chance.

He's also a fan of trees, and he pulls big branches off and nibbles the leaves. I've got a list of poisonous things he can't eat and I'm very careful with what he gets hold of. If he's eating a plant and I'm not sure what it is, I'll panic and try and take it out of his mouth. He'll battle with me and he'll be chewing it as fast as I'm trying to pull it out. He chomps really fast when he knows I don't want him to eat things.

I also have to limit his apple intake. When Alf has too much fruit he starts farting and it's *so* obvious. The other day I stood next to Alf tying my shoelace when our postman walked up. Alf farted just as I stood up and the postman laughed and said, 'Was that you?' I swear he does it on purpose (Alf, not the postman).

He's a really good sleeper and nowadays if I try to get him up before seven a.m. he gets in a right tizzy. He moves really slowly like it's a massive inconvenience for him to be awake.

There have been times when I've had to put his head collar on and drag him out of his stable because he would much rather be in the warm. It's even worse in winter. He'll still be cozied up at nine a.m. and when I try to get him out he'll look at me as if to say, 'Forget it, it's cold out there.'

Sometimes I'll watch him on the night camera after I put him in for the day. As soon as he's had his dinner he'll go and stand in a corner and he goes straight off to sleep. It still seems strange that horses sleep standing up most of the time. It's all to do with their survival instincts because they want to be able to escape quickly if a predator approaches.

Because Alf's so lazy he'll lie down if the mood takes him. For some reason he always puts his tail into his water bucket first. Then I'll see him shuffling around and down he goes. There are times when he'll wait for me to go in the following morning and help him up because he's even too lazy to do that on his own.

He's like a teenage boy and he probably sleeps more than he should. He's quite active during the day but he sometimes has a sleep in his field. If he's really tired in the afternoon he'll ask to go to bed early. I'll hear him whinnying so I'll go and see what's wrong and he'll nudge me until I let him go into his stable. I swear if I gave him the chance he'd happily snuggle in my bed.

Alf loves being inside. We've got a log cabin in the garden and if someone's in there he'll hop up the steps and saunter in so he can warm himself against the fire. When it had just been built Dad laid some wet cement outside and Alf, being Alf, went and trod in it while it was still wet. There were all these tiny hoof prints everywhere and Dad had to go over it all again.

One day Mum and I were in the cabin relaxing. I was having a cup of tea and Mum was painting, when Alf wandered in as if it was the most natural thing in the world. Mum popped out and Alf started sniffing all her paint palettes, and then knocked a massive tray of them over. He started walking around in all the paint so his feet, his nose and his belly were covered. I had to use turps to clean the floorboards but the paint still left a stain. Meanwhile, Alf was a multi-coloured mess, and he had a green streak in his mane for a couple of weeks afterwards. I think he thought it looked quite cool during his brief stint as a hipster pony!

Alf also knocked over a massive pot of varnish when my dad was painting the garden furniture on the patio. As well as covering all the paving, Alf got it on himself and I had to prise him off one of the chairs. I had to wash him so I got loads of buckets full of warm water (and some bubbles to soften the blow) and I spent over an hour trying to get all the varnish out. As soon as I'd finished he went into his field and rolled around in the mud so he was absolutely filthy. I stood there watching him doing it knowing I couldn't do anything. It was like he was saying, 'you give me a bath, this is what you get.'

My parents are really understanding about Alf being a free-range pony and getting to go where he wants to, and they let Alf get away with murder. A lot of the time I'm really the one to blame because I'll have let him go somewhere he shouldn't. I hold my hands up and say that nine times out of ten it's my fault.

I've let him into the house several times when my parents have been out or away and it's always ended in disaster. When Mum and Dad went on holiday he came in and rolled all over Mum's brand-new rug. I spent six days cleaning it, trying to get out the mud stains, but even now they're slightly visible.

Another time he smashed my mum's favourite vase and left a dirt stain on one of the carpets because his hooves were muddy. I was going to try and blame it on my brother or the dogs. My parents said to me, 'Hannah, has Alf been in the house?' I looked in the other direction and very unconvincingly said, 'Noooooo.'

However I totally stitched myself up when I uploaded a photo of Alf having fun in our living room. It didn't cross my mind that my parents would see it. They're not into social media and I didn't know they check my Little Alf page, but I was wrong. I got a message from Dad that simply said, 'You've been busted.'

Alf has been in to watch TV with me a few times since but I always clean his hooves first. He knows we keep a big bag of carrots in the kitchen so he always makes a beeline for them when I sneak him in. He's also wise to the fact that there's always a packet in the fridge (they're for humans but Alf doesn't mind about that) so he'll go over and nudge the door with his nose waiting for me to open it. Of course I give in, and one Sunday when Mum went to make the roast she realised half the bag was missing. I think we're a bad influence on each other.

Alf doesn't mind being outside when the weather is good, but given the choice he's not really an all-weather horse. When the sun is out he runs around with a smile on his face. I'll often sit in the fields with the horses for hours when the weather is nice so he associates sun with me being around.

He's not keen on me leaving him outside overnight in the summer. Sometimes his stable gets too hot when the weather is good – it's like a greenhouse, so I have no choice but to leave him in his field. The following morning he'll give me proper dagger eyes and he won't let me stroke him or anything. It really upsets me but it's for the best. One time he was so cross the next day he ignored me for hours, and then he picked up one of my trainers and ran off with it, refusing to give it back. I think he was punishing me.

On the plus side, last summer I started making all the horses lollies, which they loved. Alf was forever trying to steal my Magnum lollies but I knew they would be bad for him, so I suddenly got this idea of making him his own lollies. I Googled it to try and find a recipe but I couldn't find one anywhere, so I decided to get creative and make up my own by blending up water, carrots and apples. They were so simple and easy to do but they looked really good. I also made a batch where I put chopped-up fruit in without blending it and they looked so cool.

I went into town and got the biggest moulds I

could find. Someone said to me, 'Are you making some lollies to treat yourself in this hot weather?' and I replied, 'No, I'm making some for my horses, actually.' I'm sure they thought I'd lost it.

I made a video as I was preparing them and I posted it on YouTube and it seemed to kick off a bit of a craze. Lots of horse websites and forums started sharing, and all of a sudden tons of people started sending me pictures of the horse lollies they'd made. Someone made a massive block using an empty ice cream tub, which would have been Alf's dream come true.

As soon as I took them out to the horses they went crazy. Alf in particular. He was jumping up and trying to nick them all out of my hand and they went down a storm. Once Alf had finished his he started trying to nick Paddy's, but he wasn't having any of it.

I made a batch of banana ones next because bananas are good for horses, but Alf turned his nose up at them. I put in this really nutritious powder that makes horses' coats shiny and Alf hated it, so I think he rumbled me. I reckon he smelt it and got wise to it. There really is no fooling him. I had been thinking that I could put his worming medicine in a lolly next time I need to give it to him, but after seeing his reaction to the lollies I don't think there's any chance I would get away with it. He'd probably spot what I was trying to do a mile off.

I have to fill the horses' water buckets up much more regularly in summer, and Alf has two four-gallon water buckets in his field to make sure he never goes thirsty. It's hard work filling them up and carrying them down from the main water tap, and Alf used to have a terrible habit of knocking them over so the water spilled out everywhere the minute I got them in place. He went through a really bad phase of doing it and I'd end up exhausted from traipsing up and down so many times. Nowadays I put the buckets in two huge tyres, so even though he still tries to nudge them over with his nose, they absolutely won't budge.

He really hates wind and we do get some cracking storms in the Dales. If they're really bad they can almost blow him off his feet. I've had to go and rescue him from high winds and put him in his stable because I'm worried about him being carried off by a huge gust. The only thing he likes about it being windy is the fact he can run along swishing his mane all over the place, like he's in a hair advert, and he likes it when the leaves fall of the trees so he can chase them and eat them.

He loves spring, because he likes watching the lambs at the bottom of the field. There were loads of them last spring and he kept going down and whinnying at them and licking their noses. He stood watching them for ages and they were jumping around excitedly.

He can't stand rain and being wet. If he sees a black cloud he gets really annoyed and shouts to ask to be put back in, just in case it rains. He definitely senses it. I think he's got some kind of in-built weather monitor. He'll go over to his gate ready to be taken inside and I'll look out of the window and think, what's he doing? It's not raining. Then five minutes later it will start chucking it down.

If I'm out when it starts raining and he gets wet he gets so cross with me. It's one of the worst things I can do to him. If the weather gets bad and I'm not near home I have to phone my parents and ask if one of them can run out and put Alf in his stable otherwise I know he'll be steaming.

If there's no one around to help out and he does get rained on it's like the world's ended. I'll put him back in his stable the minute I get home but he'll still give me the death stare and won't kiss me. I'll try to dry him off with a towel but he's usually in such a bad mood he walks away and won't let me near him. He'll stand in the corner of his stable and ignore me. You'd think he'd be used to rain because he spent eight months living outside in all weathers when he was first born, but he's become soft. It's probably my fault because when he was young I'd put him inside whenever the weather was bad so I probably taught him that rain is bad.

Alf hates water in general – when I bath him he'll sulk for hours. I tried to bath him when I first got him and he was running around shaking his head at me and making all sorts of ridiculous noises.

The only thing he likes about rain is puddles and mud and he'll happily roll around in them. Usually just after I've washed and brushed him. He leaves me no choice but to hose him down but he eyeballs me like I'm worst person in the world. It's funny because he enjoys getting his fur caked in dirt but he's not keen on getting his hooves dirty. If it's really boggy in his field he tiptoes around like a little prince trying to keep them clean.

He didn't know what to make of snow the first time he saw it. He seemed quite annoyed by it. The first time it snowed after I got him, I tried to get him to go outside so I could take a photo but he didn't like the idea at all. It was like he didn't trust it. He'd poke his head out of his stable, look at it, and then retreat inside. He seems to quite like it now. He doesn't like having cold hooves but I think he's realised snow can be quite fun.

Alf and I do a lot of exploring and we often go for walks. One of his favourite places to go is the wood where he likes picking dandelions with his teeth. He also enjoys eating grass, nettles and weeds, and paddling in the stream near our house.

Because of his size it's easy enough to take him for a stroll around my village (apart from when it was raining, obviously). There are only about six or seven houses and everyone knows Alf. Our local pub, the Queen's Head, even follows him on Twitter. But I do have to keep an eye on him at all times.

The first time I ever took him into the village he managed to break away from me and climb over some mini fencing into someone's garden. I was desperately trying to drag him away but he planted his feet firmly on the grass and would not move. I was pulling on his head collar as hard as I could and getting very hot and bothered and out of breath. Just as I shouted, 'Come on, Alf, this is someone else's garden,' the owners pulled into the driveway and saw this little horse trespassing on their land. I was hugely apologetic and I could feel my face getting redder and redder. Thankfully they laughed and were so good about it, even though there were lots of little hoof marks across their lawn. Nowadays they love Alf so much that they sometimes give him carrots when we walk past their house. Somehow, he always manages to win people over.

There's an egg hut in the village where you can go and pop your money in a slot and then carry your free-range eggs away. I told Mum really proudly I was going to go and get some for dinner, so I took Alfie down there and got a big tray of thirty.

I got them all the way home without breaking a single one, and I was so excited about how nice they looked I put them down on the step outside the house and shouted to Mum to come and have a look. I'd turned around for about two seconds, and turned back to see Alf flip over the entire tray with his nose and they all toppled over and smashed. I felt so bad for the chickens! The new drive had only just been laid and it was covered in broken eggs, so I had to spend ages cleaning it up. And to make things worse, we couldn't have omelettes for dinner as planned.

One time there was an old 1940s car parked

outside the pub. It was so beautiful and glossy and it must have been worth a fortune. My phone buzzed so I reached into my pocket to get it, and when I looked back up literally seconds later, Alf was happily rubbing his bum against this car. He had his nose up in the air and he was so happy. I had to drag him away while picking off a little bit of horse hair from the bonnet. The owner came out from the pub at that exact moment, and he smiled affectionately at Alf and then got in his car as if nothing had happened. He must have seen what Alf but he didn't seem to mind at all.

Another time when we went for a stroll, I could tell Alf was in the mood for mayhem, and yet for some reason I convinced myself he'd be OK. The Queen's Head's garden is always really well looked after and they have a gardener who comes in and themes it according to the seasons. They'd just replanted everything and Alf pulled up all the shrubs in the plant pots and started biting the heads off the flowers. I had to drag him away so he didn't ruin the entire display.

In spring 2017, I was fined fifty pounds because Alf was a nature vandal again. We'd just been given a grant to plant loads of daffodils in the village, which isn't a great idea because they were all along the verges of the single-track roads. Cars and tractors have to go up them to pass each other so they're always getting crushed.

Alf and I were going for a walk and I heard a car coming so I moved him up the verge. He started ripping the heads off the daffodils but there was nowhere else I could take him to get away from them because they were covering the entire area.

This car came zooming up, which is really dangerous because there are always kids playing out and people riding horses. You're supposed to drive at twenty miles an hour on our roads but this car was going at least fifty.

When he saw Alf and me the driver slammed on his brakes and wound down his window. He leant over and shouted to me, 'It's people like you that ruin our countryside. You equestrian types wreck it for us all. I work for the council and I'm going to report you.'

I was really taken aback, and then a week later I got a letter on official letter headed paper saying I had to pay fifty pounds for the daffodils Alf ruined. I have no idea how the man knew who I was and where I lived, but I'd say Alf was probably a bit of a giveaway.

I did pay the fine because I understood the reasons behind it, but that man should have got a fine for speeding, too. He was being totally reckless and putting people and wildlife at risk.

To be fair Alf does cause havoc in the village so maybe it will teach him a lesson. I gave him a good telling off and he didn't get his usual big bag of carrots from the Friday market that week.

One of the houses in the village is mainly used as a holiday home and since Alf is very instinctive, when we walk down the street he seems to know whether people are in or out. If they're in he won't cause trouble in their gardens, but if they're not he goes for it.

When I saw the postman the other day he eyed Alf really suspiciously and said, 'You know the chain wires keep coming off the wooden posts at the front of the garden of Wish Cottage, don't you?' There was no point in denying it was Alf. I'm constantly putting the chains back up and Alf is constantly knocking them down again. If there's no one staying in the holiday home there's no risk of getting caught, so he's in his element.

Another one of my neighbours mows his lawn every week and he's so proud of his perfect grass. He's got special wire around it so animals can't get in.

I was walking Alf on his lead rope and chatting to a lady I know when she said, 'Should Alf be in there?' When I turned round he'd climbed over the wire and was helping himself to some shrubs. I didn't want to alert the owner to the fact that Alf was squashing his lawn so I had to clamber over and try to drag him back out through the gate. The neighbour was away so I thought we might get away with it, but then I realised Alf had left a line of his signature hoof prints across the grass so it was only a matter of time before I got another knock at my door.

Alf doesn't have a standard shaped hoof. Horses usually have soft tissue called a frog, which is triangle in shape, that's linked together, and it balances them as they walk. Alf doesn't have that so his foot is flat and it looks more like a circle. People don't under-stand how he can stand upright because his hoof is only about the size of a two pound coin. He's quite stocky so how he balances on these ridiculously small things is a mystery.

Horses' hooves have to be trimmed every twelve weeks and the farrier struggles to pick Alf's feet up to trim them because he can tip over so easily. Alf hates having his hooves trimmed and he always whips his head round and tries to bite the farrier's bum. The only bit he'll stand still for is the polish at the end. The farrier uses special hoof oil which makes them nice and shiny and Alfie seems to like that. I guess it goes back to him being vain about his appearance – it's like a horse manicure . . .

He's not happy when he has to have his worming treatment either. Like dogs and cats, horses have to have medicine twice a year to ward off potentially fatal worms. But rather than have a simple tablet like other animals, horses have it in paste form.

At sixty pounds a tube, it's not cheap. The last time I gave it to Alf he spat it out. When I gave him a second tube he did the same. That's a hundred and twenty pounds of medicine down the drain! Or rather, on the stable floor. Thankfully I'd prepared the second time around and I'd put some paper down to catch it. I was able to scoop it up and to coax him into swallowing it by giving him a carrot at the same time.

I don't want it to sound like Alf is naughty all the time because he's really not. Just most of the time. And he does generally really like people too, but I think he gets scared sometimes because everyone is so much bigger than him. Unless he knows their walk really well it's hard for him to recognise people. He tends to know who people are because of their shoes, and he really likes it when people bend down so he can see their faces. He also likes small children because they're often the same height as him, although he's not very keen when they start clambering all over him.

I went back to hospital for the follow-up appointment about my back at the end of summer 2014 and the doctors were really happy with my progress. They were amazed by how far I'd come, and it was mainly as a result of doing sit-ups and yoga-type exercises. My parents bought me a core machine so I used that twice a day and that helped massively. I still use it now and I can easily do five hundred sit-ups in a morning, which isn't something I ever thought I'd be able to say!

If I don't do my exercises regularly I really notice how quickly my body changes. If I let things slip I'll soon be in pain again, so even when I'm feeling lazy (Christmas is always tough!) I have to keep on top of things.

Even now my back still clicks sometimes, but I've been told that as the years go on muscle will start to grow around it so that should stop eventually.

That summer was a great one for me but it was also a bit tricky at times. My friends were on holiday from college so I should have been seeing a lot more of them, but it didn't really work out like that. Obviously when I left college initially I didn't see my friends as much anyway. And because they were with each other every day they'd often go out straight from college and I kind of got forgotten about. Plus, I was working a lot, so I didn't have as much free time as them.

The bottom line was that my friends weren't getting in touch as much as they had been and it was quite a lonely time. In the past if I'd been upset about something like that I would have gone riding to get it out of my system, but that wasn't possible anymore. Of course I had this amazing little creature to fill the void but I was coming up for eighteen and I felt like I should have been going out drinking and clubbing at least some of the time.

I was waiting for the urge to dress up and start partying to kick in but it just didn't. I'd get invited out in the evening by mates every now and again but I was either working or tired from looking after the horses and I really didn't fancy it. When friends talk about nights out they have I still wonder if

I'm missing out. I went through a phase where I convinced myself I should be more sociable. I used to watch shows like *Geordie Shore* and think, is that what everyone my age gets up to? So I gave it a go, but I didn't have these mind-blowing nights out that everyone else seems to have. I actually found it all pretty boring.

The nearest club to me is miles away so the few times I did go out I didn't get in until about six a.m. the following morning. I was so tired, all I wanted to do was lie around like a blob and move as little as possible. I'd have to force myself to go and spend time with the horses and then get back on the sofa as soon as I could.

Not surprisingly my partying experimentation didn't last long. I've only had a few hangovers in my life and they've been so awful I would happily never have one again. I did get a bit of pressure and one friend would message me saying 'Stop spending all your time with Alf and come out!' She didn't mean it in a horrible way; I think she wanted me to have fun.

Alf is my priority, one hundred per cent. I think if my life had gone in more of a party direction I may have lost interest in my horses, or not had the energy to look after them as well as I wanted to. Also, if I had planned to go to university I definitely would have thought twice about rescuing Alf because there would be no one to look after my animals, so my life would be completely different.

I'll always choose a night in over a night out, and generally by eight p.m. I'll be in my pyjamas messing around on my laptop and editing videos. I'll watch TV with my family or we'll listen to our jukebox (a birthday present from my mum to my dad a couple of years ago).

I'll also watch a lot of YouTubers, especially equestrian ones, because it's nice to see what everyone else is doing. I might Google editing tips because I enjoy learning new things, and I also do a lot of writing in the evenings. I've got a weekly column in the *Yorkshire Times* so I'm always jotting down ideas for that.

Quite often my rabbits and guinea pigs will come into the house and hang out at night. I tend to dedicate my days to the big animals and the evenings to the little ones. It may all sound pretty boring to some people but my lifestyle totally suits me.

I have to get up at six thirty a.m. every day to muck all four horses out, feed them and put them out in the field, but I enjoy it. A lot of people ask me if I get sick of doing the same thing day after day but I really don't. I love looking after my horses and taking care of them. They're all incredible in their own way.

On a typical day with Alf I'll get up, put the kettle on, make a tea and wander down the yard (Alf likes tea too, so I have to be careful of mine). I'll take the dogs down and get Alfie out. He'll give me a kiss and then follow me to the tack room. He always likes looking to see what's in my mug, and if it's cold enough he'll shove his nose in it and have a little sip. I know, it's a bit disgusting!

Once the horses are fed I'll let them all out, and Alf will go into his paddock, and probably try and wind the other horses up a bit. He'll follow me around as I fill up all the water butts in the fields, and he often sits by my side like a dog. That generally takes about an hour.

We usually do some clicker training in the morning because that's when he's more awake, but if he's not in the mood he'll let me know by biting my shoes or wandering off. If he *is* in the mood we'll practise doing 'kiss', standing on a block or going over some mini jumps.

Next I'll feed the rabbits and guinea pigs and he'll come with me. They quite like him now. He'll go over and sniff them and they'll give him a little sniff back.

Alf gets a brush every day and then we'll go for a walk down the road and he'll say hello to any other horses we bump into. He'll also eat daffodils, of course, which he's *not* allowed to do.

We've had to change the times of our walks now. We have so many people stopping us, it can take us two hours just to get round the village, which is only about two miles. The other day we set off at three p.m., and so many of my neighbours stopped us we didn't get back home until six, and it's only a mile. A total of sixteen people stopped us (I counted!). One lady brought out some carrots for us, then some builders even stopped us and asked if this was 'famous Alf'. I have no idea how they knew who he was. They were the last people I thought would be interested in Alfie.

When we get home, Alf will have his dinner, which is horse feed, haylage and water, and then he'll have a nap for a couple of hours. He does the same every day, and I swear one day I'll go in there and find him snuggled up with a face mask on and earplugs in.

At about ten thirty p.m., I'll go down to the yard with the dogs and a hot chocolate. Then I'll sit with him and groom him and brush him before I go to bed.

We do have a bit of a routine we stick to because Alf seems to like it that way, but some days we'll have different things on, like a book signing or an event or some visitors, so no two days are ever exactly the same. Obviously, whatever the day holds, it will *always* involve him doing something naughty or cute.

Just when I think nothing can surprise me something else happens. The other morning I gave Alfie his breakfast and put him in his field. I shut the gate and when I turned round two crows were sitting on his back pulling out his loose hair. They started flying back and forth to our barn and they were obviously using his fur to build a nest. It was so lovely to watch and special moments like that are worth every bit of hard work.

Chapter 7

Pony Tales

As October 2014 approached, I prepared to officially launch my first book. It finally felt like the right time. I'd been a bit lacking in confidence and thinking, should I, shouldn't I?, but then I decided to go for it. I ordered twenty copies and crossed my fingers people would like it.

I wrote about the book on my blog, and I also mentioned it on social media, and all twenty copies sold in a couple of days. That gave me the drive to order more, and I got a real buzz when good reviews started coming in. I loved the fact that both kids and adults were enjoying something that had come entirely from my imagination. I wanted to start work on my second book as soon as possible.

Because I'd been working so hard I'd managed to save up some money and was able to finance printing the books myself. I didn't make fortunes from it or anything, and certainly not enough to live on, but the fact that I was making money from doing something I loved was very exciting.

Jeanette, my boss at Quaint and Quirky, suggested that we started to stock my book in the store and they proved really popular. Whenever people bought a copy I was always too embarrassed to tell them that I'd written it. If customers saw that the author was local they'd start to ask questions. I'd tell them all about 'Hannah' without mentioning I was her. One lady once said to me, 'She sounds amazing!' and I smiled broadly and replied, 'Yes, she's a nice girl!'

I was once telling a family about Hannah and Alf and one of the kids flicked through the book. She caught sight of the photo of me at the back and said, 'But isn't that you? It looks like you?' I denied it because I felt shy but I don't think I was fooling anyone.

I had to get over my bashfulness when Jeanette came up with the idea of doing some 'meet the author' days. If I was working she'd offer people the chance to come in and get their book signed so I started selling loads more because of that.

I started thinking about different way of marketing the book. I really wanted to get my name out there so that more people would know about *The Discovery of the Wild Pony*. I started marketing the book via social media, using both mine and Alfie's accounts. I posted regular updates and told people where they could buy it from. It was a pretty basic marketing plan but I got an incredible reaction.

I got an email from another shop in the local area that asked me to send over the wholesale prices. The day I got the email I was so excited I was desperate to tell someone but no one else was at home so I had to jump up and down on my own, and then go and share the news with Alf. Later the same day I logged on to my email and I had loads of messages from other shops that wanted to place orders. I was so shocked I had to keep refreshing the page to make sure it was real.

I made the decision to invest my savings in a big print run. It was a big risk because the shops were taking them on a sale or return basis, so I'd only get paid if the books sold. If sales dried up I'd be left with boxes of books and an empty bank account. But if I hadn't taken the risk I would never have known how things would turn out, and then I'd always have wondered.

My family and friends were so supportive of my new venture but there were some people who thought the fact that I'd written a book was a bit ridiculous. One girl said to a friend of mine, 'What's Hannah doing with her life? She's never going to make a living out of that.' I also got a lot of spiteful comments from people I know (and some I don't) on Twitter. All I could do is put it down to jealousy because I've never done anything to hurt or upset anyone.

It was like some people thought I had ideas above my station or I reckoned I was something special, but that was so far from the truth. Anyone who heard nasty things being said about them would feel the same. I used to get really hurt when people said something unkind about me, but it was ten times worse if they said something mean about Alf. That used to make me angry because he can't defend himself.

They say success is the best revenge and I have to say the more copies my book sold, the more indifferent I became to people's negative opinions. It still stung when they said mean things sometimes, but instead of letting it get to me I put all my energy into planning my next work move. The most important thing was that I kept faith in myself.

I invested a thousand pounds on stock, which is a hell of a lot of money when you're seventeen and you've had to work day and night for it. Thankfully the books started selling really well and shops began ordering more copies. Because I was able to print on demand I was using the money I'd earned from book sales to print more, while also making a bit of profit.

Word started to spread about the book and I got asked to do some magazine and newspaper interviews. My first one was for the *Darlington and Stockton Times*, my local newspaper. I was so excited but I kept worrying I'd say the wrong thing or put my foot in it.

The same journalist had interviewed me before because I'd done a lot charity work a few years earlier and been given a special award: in 2013 I made five hundred Smarties biscuits for Children in Need. The school then donated a load of cakes and I sold the lot, making two and a half thousand pounds in the process. That wasn't even the only time I was in the paper that year! A few months later I scaled the equivalent of Mount Everest on our school climbing wall to raise money for another children's charity. We climbed from eight thirty a.m. until seven thirty p.m. and Rachel McKenzie, the world Thai-boxing champion, came and climbed it alongside us. I also did a skydive with my dad in 2016. We dropped from fifteen thousand feet and it was such an adrenaline rush. My poor dad was so nervous, bless him, but I would definitely do it again. We raised fifteen hundred pounds for RP Fighting Blindness, which is a really important charity to me because my nan has been losing her sight for the past twelve years now. They're only a small charity so we wanted to do something to help. I've always enjoyed putting on fundraising events. There are so many people in the world that need a helping hand, and it really doesn't hurt to do what you can. I felt really motivated after seeing what can be achieved if people pull together.

The guy who wrote the first piece saw on my blog that I'd released a book so he asked if I'd do an interview about it. An agency called Northern Press picked up on my story and I got featured in magazines like *Take a Break* and on lots of websites. It was great because more people more started to buy the book. I felt so proud that it was out there and people were learning all about Alf. It also showed the people who were sceptical about whether I was ever going to release it that I meant business and I was taking it seriously.

Because I could see the impact all the press was having I wanted to be as proactive as possible. I wrote to a couple of big horse magazines telling them my story and they ended up writing about Alf and the book too. My sales had already been nudging towards the thousands and they were going up and up. Everything I'd hoped would happen finally was, and all my hard work felt more than worth it.

I've always loved helping out charities and just after I launched my first book I became involved with an incredible one called the Riding for the Disabled Association, also known as the RDA. The kids and adults who are involved with the charity have autism or disabilities and the connections they make with the horses are incredible. When they're riding you can see such a difference in them. The RDA has been going for over forty years and there are over five hundred volunteer groups across the UK. They help twenty-eight thousand people a year, which is incredible.

I've seen other people's lives totally turned around by contact with animals. I read a really interesting book called *The Power of Horses to Heal: Riding Home* that says it's been proven horses can heal people's hearts and help those who have had trauma. After seeing the difference in the people who come along to the RDA I totally believe that. I started working with them in autumn 2014. I knew there was a branch near me so I spoke to the manager who said they were really short on volunteers. I was so keen to get started doing whatever I could to help, but I had to be CRB checked first.

Once I was finally cleared I got accepted as a volunteer. The following Thursday I set my alarm for six a.m., went and saw to the horses and then headed off, excited about what the day would bring.

I arrived at a barn, which doubled as a reception, at eight a.m. and met the head volunteer, Julia. She introduced me to another volunteer who talked me through everything, from what I could expect to where I could make a cup of tea, which is obviously very important. The centre is surrounded by fields and is an everyday riding school most days but on

Thursdays the RDA hire it out so their groups can use the facilities. It's got loads of stables, an indoor ménage, and an information office.

That first morning we went to the tack room and got the ponies ready and then we set up the arena. Different groups of kids and adults arrived every twenty minutes and it was incredible to see how happy being around the horses made them. Some of the riders have mental health issues and others had physical disabilities. There was a girl who had lost a leg through illness when she was young and she'd never imagined she'd be able to ride a horse, so to see her trotting around the ménage on a pony was just incredible. There were some kids who were quite nervous when they first arrived, but as the session went on they'd really come out of their shell and by the end they couldn't stop smiling.

A new student called Liam came along that day and I was asked to look after him. Because I was new too the other volunteers thought it would be a good combination. Liam had autism and was painfully shy, but I led him around the ménage on a Shetland and within ten minutes he started to interact with the ponies and become much chattier. His parents had looks of utter joy on their faces. His mum and dad said that since he's been riding there'd been a massive improvement in him and he chats away to them all the time now. They can't believe the difference, and it's so rewarding to watch.

After seeing the remarkably positive impact the RDA has I wanted to get involved as much as possible. The centre is run on donations, fundraising and legacies, so every pound they get is hugely important. Money is raised through anything from raffles to raft races, and associations like the People's Postcode Lottery contribute as well. But it's really down to the centres to help to generate the funds they need. I came up with the idea of donating a percentage of every book I sold to the RDA, and it's something I still do now. I save all the money up and then every six months I make a donation to help the RDA continue its incredible work.

After I'd been at the centre for a couple of weeks I suggested taking Alf along to meet the kids. They wouldn't be able to ride him but I thought they'd really enjoy being around him anyway. He was amazing with them from the word go, and they thought he was very funny and sweet.

I still take him along with me when I go and the kids spend time brushing and stroking him. There's one lad called Joe who is in a wheelchair, and while he was brushing him one time Alf started nudging his chair. I told him to stop but then I heard this crashing sound and Alfie had managed to push poor Joe's wheelchair over. Thankfully Joe and his carer found it hilarious, but ever since then I've watched him more closely. I can't take my eyes off him for a minute.

Another time one of the volunteers was teaching a group of kids about horses and giving them safety tips. Alf was tied to a post and he was supposed to be having some quiet time out. He stood in the corner right near where I was working, so every time I walked past him he started whinnying really loudly. He was making everyone giggle but he was distracting the kids so I had to go and stand with him to keep him quiet.

At the end of the session this boy called Chris came over to see Alf. He couldn't ride that day because he wasn't feeling up to it, so as a treat I said he could lead Alf around the ménage. Alf didn't like that one bit so he started picking up the pace, and before I knew it he was running full pelt around the ménage. Instead of being scared Chris totally embraced it and he started running too. Chris was supposed to be leading Alf round, but in the end it was Alf who was leading Chris round, and he couldn't stop laughing.

There are certain kids I'll see again and again at the centre, like a lovely girl called Sophie, who always strokes my hair and tells me how much she likes it. She always says to me, 'It's so silky soft!' and we talk about what shampoos and conditioners I've been using. Another is one of the adults who comes to the sessions, Amy, who is twenty-eight and has Down syndrome. She's incredibly confident around the horses, and so intelligent she picks everything up so quickly. Sometimes people underestimate her because she looks really young, but when they talk to her they're taken aback by how funny and articulate she is. I love seeing people's faces when they realise they've underestimated her.

Because the school runs as a standard riding school when the RDA aren't there, it can be that when we finish for the day there will be people waiting outside for lessons. As we file out our kids sometimes say hello to those waiting because they're all really friendly, and it always shocks me when people don't say hello back. In fact, some of them will even look away. That breaks my heart. Everyone should treat people how they want to be treated themselves, and they wouldn't like someone ignoring them like that.

I always come away from a session at the RDA feeling so elated. I've now got my bronze and silver Young Leaders awards and I'm working on my gold. To get the bronze award I had to do twenty hours of volunteering and a fundraising project alongside it. I used my books to raise money by doing signings. I got my silver by doing sixty hours of volunteering and writing a twelve thousand-word assignment. I also had to get eight references so there's quite a lot involved, but Alf and I have a special badge that says we're RDA qualified.

I've been working with the RDA for three years now. I used to go twice a week, but when work is busy I don't get the chance to go as much as I'd like to. I make sure Alf and I are always at events though, and I still go and help out regularly. The charity has made a difference to so many of the people who are involved in it. It certainly has to me. It's also been a huge learning curve for me and all the volunteers are really close, so it's like being part of a family.

The RDA is right next to Catterick Garrison, the biggest army base in the UK, and sometimes the soldiers come along to get help with their rehabilitation.

It's amazing to work with them and hear their stories as well.

I've recently started working with another horse charity called Brooke. They're a welfare charity that aims to improve the life of working horses, mules and donkeys in poverty, as well as the people who work with them. They do incredible work in places like Africa, Latin America and the Middle East. I retweeted one of their tweets and it got a really good response, so they asked if I'd go down to their London offices to meet them. I was going to London with my boyfriend the following week so I went in for a chat and they told about this event they were putting on, which was a mini hackathon. It involves people leading their pony for ten miles in a hundred days to raise a hundred pounds. They asked if Alf and I would front the campaign and it's such a great cause to get involved with, so I said yes.

I took some photos of Alf and they're using them for the campaign, and I speak to them on a weekly basis to see how I can help. I went to a big International Horse Trials in Bolesworth with them and did a talk to seven hundred and fifty students to raise awareness, and those kinds of things are so important.

Brooke know about my commitment to the RDA and they're aware that I can't commit as much time as I would like to because of the crossover. I would support every charity going if I could, but I would hate to end up in a situation where I'm really tied up and I'm not able to be totally engaged. I think the lesson here is not to spread myself too thinly so people don't get the best of Alf and me.

My second Christmas with Alf was brilliant and after a difficult year with my cousin Maria being unwell, my back problems, and leaving college, things felt really good. Maria was getting better, my back was less painful and I knew that leaving college was one of the best decisions I'd ever made.

My book was still selling well and I was getting amazing feedback from friends and family and online. If I got any nasty comments I used them to drive myself forward instead of letting them bother me.

I'd had a good year of rehabilitation and physio on my back and although I still got pains if I tried to do too much, I wanted to see if all my hard work meant I may be OK to ride again. A few days after Christmas I decided to go out on Paddy and see how it felt. I must admit, I loved it. I was really confident and thought that maybe my back really had healed thanks to all the core exercises I'd been doing. But it wasn't long before the familiar aches kicked in and it got so bad I had to turn around and head for home. According to my doctors riding has such a bad effect on me because my hips get stretched out, which is quite common in people who ride a lot. That really affects my back, and since there's only one way to sit on a horse that's something I can't do a lot about.

Sadly that day made it very clear to me that I would never be able to ride again. I'm lucky that Paddy isn't a huge fan of being ridden anymore. If he'd been a highbred horse who needed riding every day, which some do, I would have had to think about what to do long term. It wouldn't have been fair to keep him when no one was riding him. Thankfully he's very happy to hang out in his field these days, and we do training and tricks together to keep him busy and active.

To keep myself busy I decided to look into securing some book signings in the New Year. I had already been asked to go along to some book festivals and events, and by mid-January Alf and I had a packed diary for 2015. We had two book events and signings every month for the entire year. I also managed to get my books stocked in a big equestrian chain called Millbry Hill, so it was an incredible start to the year.

Millbry Hill invited us along to do a book signing in their Stokesley branch and I made sure Alf was looking his best for his big day. I brushed him and polished his tiny hoofs. Although I was nervous that no one would turn up, this felt like a really big deal for us. I set off for the first date of 'Alfie's Book Tour' with hope in my heart!

My poor parents used to drive Alf and I around everywhere. We transported Alf to the store in my dad's work van, which he had converted to make it safe for Alf to travel in. Dad put up wooden panels and we filled the back of with loads of blankets and pillows. He made a ramp so Alf could climb into the back of the van easily, but he wasn't keen. I tried to entice Alf onto it using my now failsafe method of feeding him carrots and Polos, but he still wasn't having any of it. Alfie is surprisingly strong and if he doesn't want to do something he won't. End of story. In the end Dad had to pick him up and put him in the back of the van. Once he was in there and realised how cosy it was he settled straight away. Typical Alf.

In the summer months I can lift Alf myself, but in winter he puts on weight and he's much heavier. He puts on weight because he's not out in the field as much. Often horses will lose weight in winter because their bodies are working hard to keep them warm, so their cold weather feed has more sugar and nutrition. However, Alf seems to skip the whole 'losing weight to keep warm' thing, and even though I'm really careful not to overfeed him, he ends up a bit chubbier. Because of his height, even when he's slim, poor Alf looks quite chunky in photos. It's not until people see him they realise how ridiculously tiny he is. Whatever the season, it's not ideal for someone with a bad back to lift him when he's at his lightest, let alone his heaviest.

Alf does lose weight pretty quickly, and he doesn't mind at all when he's a bit curvier than normal. Because he's very fluffy it's hard to notice, and he's very comfortable and happy with himself generally. He's got saggy skin around his bum and legs because his skin kept on growing when he didn't, but he embraces it. In winter you can't see his loose skin because he's so fuzzy, but in summer when he loses his coat it wobbles around behind him when he walks. He still thinks he's the Liam Hemsworth of the horse world, though.

I do have to be vigilant because he's very greedy. Sometimes I'll look at him and think 'he's put a bit on' and I have to up the exercise. Because I've got long legs I walk quite fast, which means Alf has to trot to keep up with me, which is great exercise for both of us really. There was a period of two months last year when we noticed that loads of the horse nuts were going missing. I said to Mum one day, 'Have you been feeding the horses? Their nuts keep disappearing.' She hadn't been near them, so it was really confusing.

The mystery was solved quicker than expected when later that day I went into the tack room and found Alf with his nose in his nuts. I said to him, 'What do you think you're doing?' and he looked up at me, held my gaze, and then went back to eating them as if he was saying, 'Just try and stop me'. I was really baffled about how he'd managed to get in the tack room because the door is on a hinge so it's always closed. When I looked back over the CCTV I realised that every time there was a strong gust of wind it blew the door open and Alf was taking his chances and running in!

I'd been worried Alf was poorly because he hadn't been eating all of his normal food, which is very unlike him, but it was no wonder when he'd been filling himself up with nuts. I had to put him on a diet and take him for more walks so he could get his bikini body back.

The best present I can give Alf is a horse lick. They look like a huge lollipop and they're really nutritious and full of vitamins and minerals. They're also quite calorific so if any horse has them too often they'll put on weight. All my horses share the licks. As soon I get one out they all smell it and they'll all be there waiting for their turn. Paddy is naughty and instead of licking them he bites big chunks out of them like they're a bar of chocolate. He'll wander around with it in his mouth all day looking very pleased with himself.

Paddy is very food oriented in general, but a couple of years ago he came unstuck after eating something he shouldn't have. He was standing at the bottom of his field and he wouldn't come up for his feed, so I knew instantly something was wrong. I walked down to put his head collar on it and tried to get him to walk up the field but he was really lethargic. I managed to get him to his stable but it took ages and I was in tears because I was so worried about him. He just wasn't himself at all.

My mum rang the vet and he came out straight away and examined him. He said it looked like he'd had a bad reaction to a plant he'd eaten. He had the early symptoms of colic, which can kill horses within twenty-four hours. It's one of the worst diseases a horse can get. We were so lucky we caught it early. The vet had to give Paddy an antibiotic injection but he couldn't find a vein, which was very worrying. It took him about ten minutes to get the drugs into him. Paddy needed the medication in his system within an hour or he could have gone downhill very rapidly. We had such a small window to save him.

We waited for Paddy to perk up but he wasn't showing any signs of recovery so he had to have a second injection. I stayed with him until it got dark and then went inside the house and watched him on CCTV. I was terrified he was going to lie down. If a horse lies down when it's ill you basically know it's going to die.

Thankfully by the next morning Paddy was almost back his normal self. It was such a relief I cried again. I think he's learnt his lesson not to try and eat everything within reach.

Anyway, back to the Millbry Hill story. And it is quite a story.

Mum drove us to the store in the van. We arrived at nine thirty a.m. and set up Alf's pen. I'd bought a child's wooden playpen that was easy to put together and dismantle so I was feeling very pleased with myself.

The book signing was due to start at ten, so I got Alf in position and sat behind a table with my books piled up waiting to meet everyone. In between munching on his hay Alfie kept nudging my leg as if he was trying to reassure me. I think he could tell I was nervous.

We were only due to be at the store for an hour and they said they were expecting around fifty people to turn up. I hoped it wouldn't be overwhelming for Alf. He was used to being around people but he hadn't met so many 'fans' before.

Just before ten a.m. Mum ran over and told me there was a queue outside. The shop wasn't even open but over seventy people had already turned up to meet Alf! By the time the hour was up over a hundred people had filed through the door and they all bought books, which was brilliant. What wasn't quite as brilliant was Alf's behaviour.

The shop had a big display of horse treats, and while I was distracted with signings Alf managed to use his feet and nose to nudge his pen over to the food section and start helping himself. One minute he was right next to me, and the next he eight feet away ripping open a huge twenty-pound bag of horse nuts. They spilled all over the floor and Alf was having the time of his life. The store manager was great about it but Alf ate so many I bought the entire bag out of politeness.

I moved Alfie's pen back over to where I was sitting and told him to behave himself, but because he'd eaten so much he got terrible gas. He kept farting and it absolutely stank. The smell was so potent there was no way people wouldn't notice so I kept smiling and apologising to them all. It wasn't like Alf did it subtly, either. When he passes wind it's so loud you know about it, and even the people at the back of the queue were poking their heads round to see where the noise was coming from. I turned to him and said, 'Alfie, come on. Have some respect.' But did he care? What do you reckon?

I was so worried people would think it was me that was making such a horrible smell. One girl who over to the table kept sniffing and she looked really disgusted so I said, 'I'm sorry, he's a typical boy!' She kind of laughed, but I could tell she was keen to get away as quickly as she could.

Another little girl came over with her book, holding a bag of sweets. As I bent down to sign her book I heard her scream. I flipped my head up and saw that Alf had moved his pen again, and this time he'd managed to shuffle all the way over to this little girl and he had his nose firmly in her open bag of Haribo Tangfastics. He was swilling his tongue around and then licking his lips. I thought the girl was going to start crying so I gave her the book for free.

Our hour was nearly up, but to prevent any more mishaps two members of staff came and sat on each side of his pen to stop Alf moving again. He hated that they'd ruined his fun so he kept going over and jokingly trying to nibble them. They sat with their arms crossed trying to look serious and he was running up and nipping their elbows.

Amazingly the same store has had us back twice since so they obviously weren't too horrified by his performance, but 'buy Alf a more secure pen' went straight to the top of my to-do list.

Shortly afterwards Alf and I were invited to the Manchester Book Festival and I went armed with a new heavyweight metal pen. Alf wasn't going to mess things up this time. Once it was in place there was no way he'd be able to move so I was confident things would go without a hitch.

I set up my table next to his pen and organised the books in neat piles. I'd ordered some Little Alf merchandise to sell alongside the book – some little teddy versions of him and some china wellingtons with the Little Alf logo on them – so I arranged those nicely too.

I'd popped over to talk to one of the other stall-holders when suddenly I heard a massive clattering sound. Alf had climbed up on the bars of his pen and pushed over several piles of books and a minia-ture bookshelf I was proudly displaying on my table. Not only that, but he also sent the teddies flying everywhere, and every single one of the china wellies fell onto the floor and smashed. People very kindly rushed over to help me clear up but all I could think was 'that's hundreds of pounds worth of stock Alf's just ruined!'

I thought Alf had done his worst for the day, but there was more to come. The compere for the event walked over to Alfie and made a joke about wanting to interview him. As the compere put his microphone to Alf's mouth he bit the pop filter – the big bit of black foam – off and then dropped it onto the floor. As it landed you could see it had a big hole in it, and as the compere didn't have a replacement he couldn't use his microphone for the rest of the day. Every time he saw me he'd mention it, and I could tell he was getting more and more cross, but short of travelling into Manchester town centre to try and get him a new one there was little I could do.

Alf knew he'd gone too far that time – his face said it all. He absolutely knows when he's done something he shouldn't, you can tell because he looks really sheepish and his ears start to twitch. He'll also lower his head, and sometimes he won't look at me because he knows he's in trouble. I try so hard not to laugh because he has to learn when he's being naughty, but it's *so* hard.

The next big book signing we did was at Gosforth Community Centre in Newcastle that May. They invite eight authors to go along every year and I was one of the lucky ones. I was really surprised because it was the first thing I did that was outside of Yorkshire and I didn't expect anyone to know who we were. We were supposed to be there from ten a.m. until two p.m. but we sold out of books by midday, which was overwhelming. Alf was amazingly well behaved for once and we had such a fun day. If only Alf could be that good all the time, eh?

Chapter 8

Horsing Around

Off the back of our successful book signings I decided to do some signings at local agricultural shows and events. The first one was called Countryside Live and again Alf came along with me. I sold all of my stock, two hundred copies of *The Discovery of the Wild Pony* just at that first fair, and I couldn't believe it. It got people talking about Alf and the book and I couldn't wait to go to more events. I started getting messages from people asking where we were going to be next so they could come along and see us.

I found out about other events by searching for

listings on the internet and I got a bit overexcited and booked us into loads. I hadn't done any market research and I naively assumed that everyone would want to buy my books. I soon learnt that it was kids, parents and grandparents who were most interested, and that I needed to pick events relevant to the audience.

I went along to one show and it turned out to be a woman's conference and I stuck out like a sore thumb. I thought if I did a scatter approach I'd be fine, but that day showed me that it really wasn't like that at all. I didn't have a business model or leaflets or anything, so I didn't look very professional, and I think all the attendees wondered what on earth I was doing at such a highbrow event. The talks were about really deep issues and I was there asking, 'Would you like to buy a book about a really tiny pony?'

I didn't even have a proper website back then. I'd put one together after teaching myself basic skills but I cringe when I look back on it now. It looked like an eighteen-year-old who didn't know what they were doing had put it together – which to be fair was exactly what it was.

I decided it was wise to stick to agricultural shows

because at least I knew there would be horse fans. I wanted to start looking more professional so I had an 'Alf' marquee made up. It's black with 'Little Alf' written on the front in yellow. It goes everywhere with me now. It's very showbiz: it's got windows so I can let air in if Alf gets too hot, and I can build a pen for him inside so he feels safe. I also know he can't get into too much trouble while he's in there, which is a relief.

The first time I used the marquee things seemed a little quiet, and it was only when I put a board up outside explaining that Alf was inside that people started to show interest. Once they realised there was a live creature in the tent they were really intrigued. In the end I had to stop people joining the queue because it was so long. One girl queued for ages to see Alf and when she came in she said to me, 'What's up with him then?' I looked really confused and said, 'What do you mean? There's nothing wrong with him.' She cocked her head and said Alf looked 'weird' and 'odd'. Then she asked for a photo and to get her book signed. She posted the picture on Twitter straight away and said how lovely it was to meet us and how amazing Alf was. I just don't understand people sometimes!

That year I booked Alf and myself a stand at the East Riding Country Fair, a huge event that's hosted at the Driffield Showground. They gave us a slot in the main arena because I'd told them about all the tricks Alf could do. Alf and I did loads of preparation and while we were 'rehearsing' he was rolling his ball and standing on his block and being so obedient. I couldn't wait to show everyone what he could do.

The fair was a lot busier than I was expecting and as soon as we arrived I headed over to the main arena. While we were waiting to do our display I watched some of the other acts and my heart began to sink. The guy before us was doing a display with some incredibly well-trained gun dogs. They were like something off *Britain's Got Talent* and I thought, *this is going to be really embarrassing. We're nowhere near as good as them.*

When it was our turn I felt the weight of everyone's stares. I set up Alf's props in the middle of the arena and then led him out. He looked around at the crowd, looked at me and then just stood there refusing to move. I was encouraging him to kick the ball or climb up on his block, but every time I got hold of his head collar he backed away from me.

I tried pulling at his lead rope and he started

bucking and rearing and I went so red my face felt like it was burning. I knew I was fighting a losing battle. In the end I had to get the microphone and announce to the extremely unimpressed audience that Alfie didn't want to play that day. We were supposed to be doing another performance at four p.m. but we were politely told that we weren't needed. Lesson learnt about Alf being a show pony!

The Great Yorkshire Show in Harrogate was also interesting. Prince Charles and Camilla were the special guests and they were going around chatting to some of the stallholders. I was beside myself thinking they might come in and meet Alf. Because they had quite a big entourage Alf decided he didn't like all the noise so he started screaming his head off as they walked past. I said to him, 'Alf, that man is going to be the king of England one day. You must behave!'

Alf was always a big hit with children and a few primary schools got in touch to ask if we would visit so the pupils could meet him. We kicked off our first trip to a local school by doing a talk in the children's playground. They were all amazed by Alf, and so excited when they got to stroke him.

The teacher asked if they could show Alf their classroom and get a photo taken with their class mascot, a stuffed crocodile. They're always taking photos of him and putting them on their website. There's a school in South Africa that have exactly the same toy so they exchange pictures and stories all the time. They wanted a really special photo of Alf so they could tell their distant friends all about him. Of course I agreed straight away. What could possibly go wrong?

I walked Alf up the corridor to the classroom with all the kids following excitedly behind, and the teacher gleefully got the crocodile out of the cupboard. As soon as she walked over to Alf I saw his eyes light up. I knew what that look meant.

I said to the teacher, 'Maybe don't put the teddy near his mouth. Just put in on his head for the photo or something.' She put it on the floor in front of him instead, and then everything started to go in slow motion. Alf bent down, clamped the teddy between his teeth and started shaking it around really violently. I was standing a few feet away so I dived over to try and grab it. By the time I got there one of the crocodile's legs had come off and was flying through the air to the other side of the classroom.

I heard the teacher gasp and then two of the kids burst into tears. I felt terrible. I tried to make it better by telling the children the crocodile would be OK but I could see some of their bottom lips trembling.

Alf's jaws were firmly clamped around the crocodile like a dog with a tennis ball and I only managed to coerce him into dropping it by offering him a carrot.

I retrieved the crocodile from the floor but as I picked it up a load of the stuffing fell out, which made things ten times worse. I handed it straight back to the teacher and apologised. She recoiled in horror as she took the slobbery, injured crocodile, then, holding it by one of its remaining legs, looked me dead in the eye and said, 'We can't get another one of these.'

I took that as our cue to leave so we quickly said our goodbyes and made a beeline for the school gates. Alf wasn't in the least bit bothered by his bad behaviour, and as per usual I was the one walking away with my tail between my legs instead of him. The irony.

I logged on to the school website the following week to see if the crocodile had been nursed back to health and I saw that they'd managed to re-stuff him and sew his leg back on. I'm not sure Mr Crocodile will ever be the same again, though. I don't imagine we'll be asked to open their summer fête anytime soon.

I didn't want the awfulness of our first school visit to stop other children from experiencing the joys of Little Alf, so I went in for round two. It was another local school and the plan was for us to go into the hall so I could tell the children all about my life with Alf. Only we didn't make it that far.

As we were walking up the corridor to the assembly the school bell went off and spooked Alf so he started running off in full flight, dragging me along behind him. I was scared I was going to fall over and injure myself so I had to let go of him.

Thankfully the corridor was a dead end but once I caught up with him he refused to let me near him. He kept running from side to side, snorting and bucking. It didn't help that the kids thought it was hilarious so they were clapping and egging him on. I eventually managed to get him back under control but all the teachers were watching me open-mouthed.

We decided it was safer to go outside to the playground so I could do the talk there, but there were much more fun things for Alf to do than stand still behind me like a good boy.

First, he pulled me over to a beautiful flowerbed that the children had planted for a science project. He started chewing any flowers that took his fancy and once he was done with that he began picking up pots and smashing them.

I was frantically trying to wrestle him away when he spotted the greenhouse. Argh! The door was wide open so he dragged me in there and started nibbling at plants and eating the vegetables the kids were growing. I was trying to grab his head and pull him out but he was so determined.

We have done a couple of successful school visits, however. We went to one in Newcastle that went so well we've been invited back several times. When Alf is good, he's great, and for some reason he does me proud whenever we go there. He does his tricks and he blows kisses at the kids, which always goes down really well. I just can never tell which Alf I'm going to get when I turn up to places.

Kids of all ages write to me about Alf and so many say they'd would love to write books themselves after reading Alf's. I love the fact they're inspired by him. Kids also draw lovely pictures of Alf and send us in stories, and I often put them into his official magazine. One girl's mum emailed me to say that her daughter took the magazine to school and showed everyone her picture was featured. She thought she was dead famous, which is so cute.

In the end I was getting so many requests to send pictures and letters I set up a PO box. I mentioned it on social media but I didn't expect anything to happen straight away. The first time I opened the box there were over two hundred letters and I couldn't believe it! I was so happy. It took me a day to go through them all, and then a couple of weeks to reply to them, but I did get back to everyone who included their address. They were such lovely letters and most of them said how much they love Alf and our book. A lot were from young kids, and a lot of the parents had put in notes saying that their child really enjoys following me and Alf on social media.

I also got a lot of fan art from university students and they were amazing. I'd love to keep replying to everyone because they've taken the time to get in contact. But if things get out of control and I don't have time, I might have to get someone to help me out!

You probably think I've got no control whatsoever over Alf, and to be honest you'd be right. Alf does what Alf wants to do whether I like it or not. It's weird that I can train him to play football and pose for photos but he can't behave when he needs to. It's also strange that he understands words like 'kiss' and 'carrot', but simply can't get to grips with the word 'no'.

I do try to be strict with Alf. I really do. I used to get really embarrassed about what he got up to but as time's gone on I've got so used to it. It's who he is and I can't dampen down his personality. People are always commenting on how naughty he is but I think that's what makes him who he is. And he's wonderful.

Looking back now, the way I released my first book was pretty crazy because I didn't really know what I was doing! I was ready for round two but I felt like I needed to do more research before I released the second one.

I contacted some authors I liked and asked if they could pass on any pearls of wisdom. On Cathy Cassidy's recommendation I bought the *Writers' and Artists' Yearbook*, and Linda Chapman gave me some tips and suggested some more self-publishing and author sites I could register on. Because of this research I felt much more clued up about everything when I started writing my second book just after Christmas 2014. The main thing I'd learnt from the first was that the next one needed to be longer, and I needed to get it proofread before I got any printed up.

I knew I wanted some kind of magic to be involved again, and I wrote loads of drafts before it started to feel right. I used to write everything by hand when I first started because it felt more real that way somehow. Once I'd written it out I'd type it up and read it through about a million times changing little things here and there. I've gone straight to computer now I've become braver.

I ordered my first sample of *The Magical Adventures of Little Alf: The Enchanted Forest*, but when it arrived it just didn't look right. I'm a real perfectionist and just like when I'd initially had the first book through I wasn't totally happy with the cover. Then when I got a new copy printed I didn't like some of the wording inside. Once again I went through several versions before I was happy to unleash it onto the public.

I launched my second Alf book at an open stables day in a place called Middleham in April 2015. There were loads of beautiful racehorses there and Alf was standing in the middle of them, screaming his head off and winding them all up. Amazingly we still had a queue of people who wanted to meet him afterwards and the book sold really well.

I blogged about the new book and talked about it on social media, and I started being asked to do more press interviews. People who had bought the first book were keen to buy the second, so I already felt like things were moving along really well. I certainly hadn't turned into a publishing expert overnight but I felt like I was finding my feet.

I did several more events to publicise the book – although I was much more selective this time, and I only took Alf to things here and there if I thought he'd enjoy them and behave himself.

I was already thinking about book three, but the first and second books had been released quite close together and I didn't want to bombard people with Alf tomes, so I decided to wait another six months or so. I wanted to take my time over it and pace myself, and give myself a chance to market the first two as best as I could.

I also felt like I'd gone a bit crazy with launching branded goods and that maybe I was rushing things a bit. I'd got carried away with the Little Alf empire and I needed to take a step back.

I still had had moments where I've thought, *what am I going to do long term? How am I going to support myself? What if people stop buying the books?* I thought about studying something completely different or settling for an office job that would give me a regular wage. I know I would have hated it, but was it time to be sensible?

In the end it was my parents who turned to me and said, 'Just keep on the right track for you and you'll get there.' They were the ones who gave me the confidence to carry on and I'm so glad I did. They've been really supportive from day one. They've never told me to go out and get a proper job. Even now if I come across a bit of a bump their support is always there to help me to keep going.

I decided I wanted the third book to have a Christmas theme, which fitted in perfectly with when I wanted to release it. I absolutely love Christmas, and of course Alf arrived in my life at Christmas and he was the most amazing present ever.

Little Alf, the Magic Helper came out in October 2015. I'd passed my driving test by then so I was able to get myself around without the help of my parents, which made things much easier. It was the perfect time to do festive fairs with Alf but I didn't want to wear him out so I did smaller events, like signings at my local café. It's nice to take him to really special events with big audiences every now and again so people get to meet him and he gets showered with attention, but I do keep them to a minimum.

Alf started properly teething around this time too, which can be really painful, so he needed more time to rest. All horses, ponies and Shetlands lose their baby teeth and then get adult ones just like humans do. Horses and ponies start to lose their baby teeth when they're around two. Their teeth are supposed to grind against each other and come out on their own, but because of Alf's overshot jaw his couldn't do that. He'll shed around twenty-four baby teeth in total and it will be a long process. He won't lose all of them until he's around seven.

By the time horses are five they should have between thirty-six to forty-four fully developed adult teeth. It's hard to imagine Alf having so many because his mouth is so small.

You don't have to brush horses' teeth because a horse produces saliva that naturally cleans then, and I'm pleased because knowing Alf he'd turn it into a right drama.

It was a bit of a testing time, for both me and Alf,

though. When he first started teething he wanted to chew everything, but thankfully now some of his teeth are coming out he's getting a bit better. He was also quite grumpy when his teeth were falling out and the new ones were coming through. It can be really painful and when it is – he lets me know all about it.

We've had the vet out a few times to check on his teeth because he got little blisters on either side of his mouth and on his gums so he had to have some special treatment. The vet he said he could see how sore they were and he was surprised Alf wasn't making a bigger deal out of it. He also had to get his teeth filed down like all horses do, and he was not happy. The vet comes and checks all the horses' teeth once a year and he'll rasp them, which is when the chewing surfaces are filed down to make them smooth. All the other horses are totally fine having it done but the vet has to give Alf a mild sedative so he's calm enough to do the procedure. Afterwards Alf ignores me because he's cross about it.

The worst thing about Alf's teething problems was that he couldn't have any carrots. They were too hard for him to chew so he had to have only soft feed. A lot of people collect their horses' teeth but I could never find any of Alfie's because they're so tiny. Not that I'd know what to do with them if I did, mind!

Alf's favourite thing to chew when he's going through a bad teething phase is the top of my wellingtons. I guess it's because they're so soft. I bought a new pair of riding boots that cost me over a hundred pounds and he left teeth marks all around the top of them. The marks weren't very even so I couldn't even get away with pretending it was a cool pattern that was supposed to be on there. I was always finding Alfie teeth marks on things so I got him some baby teething rings and dog chews to keep him satisfied.

I think he's really proud that some of his adult teeth have already come through. When I say to him, 'Show me your teeth,' he'll lift up his lip and let me have a look. His back teeth have still got to come out but they should be much less painful. I really hope so. I can't deal with any more of his teenage moods.

Alf always senses when the vet is coming. He just knows. As well as his sixth sense, he also recognises his voice, so as soon as he hears it he starts whinnying. He's aware something is going to happen to him and the chances are he won't like it. We still have the same vet as the one who gelded him so Alf will probably always associate that bad experience with him. The vet is great with Alfie though. He's got two young kids and he's bought the Alf books for them, and his wife thinks Alf is amazing. I always bump into her at shows and she's so excited to see him.

The vet knows how important Alf is to me and he takes such good care of him. He's more difficult to tend to because of his size so a lot of patience (and resilience) is needed. Our vet is also very understanding about how emotional I can get. He knows how passionate I am about my animals so he won't judge me when I'm crying because one of my rabbits has got a bad paw!

Alfie has regular check-ups and the vet always says he's one hundred per cent healthy, which is the most important thing. You can tell how healthy and happy he is by his cheeky nature and the way he bolts around the fields. He has a flu jab every year and his last one was a disaster. It's especially important for Alfie to have them because his dwarfism means his immune system is a bit compromised, but he loathes injections (who doesn't?) so he'll do anything to avoid them. We had a plan for handling it this time around. The vet said to me, 'I'll hide up by the house until you can get him into his stable because I know what a handful he can be.'

I went down to his field and put his head collar on and Alf just knew. He put his brakes on and that was it. I had to crouch down and lay out a trail of carrots for him to follow so he'd move. I got him to the door of his stable where the vet was waiting to jab him there and then so it was over before Alf could realise. Unfortunately we underestimated Alf. As the vet went to put the needle in Alf whipped round and tried to kick him, so we had to go to plan B.

We got Alf inside and put him in the corner of his stable so he was trapped. The vet walked over really stealthily and tried to give him the injection, but Alf launched forward and knocked him over. The poor vet fell back and landed in a heap on the floor. The worst thing was I hadn't had time to muck out Alfie's stable that morning so there was horse poo on the ground and the vet had ended up with it all over his hands.

It took the vet three attempts to give Alf his shot. He's a pretty sturdy man who deals with full-sized horses every day of his life, and yet he was floored by twenty-eight inches of pure fury.

I've since discovered that the vet and the farrier have a secret name for Alf – the Little Monster. And considering his treatment of both of them, I do get why. The farrier let it slip when he came to do the horses' hooves a while back. He finished seeing to Badger, Paddy and Pepper and then said, 'Right, let's get the Little Monster over and done with now.' I said to him, 'What do you mean?' and he replied, 'It's what we all call Alf because he's so naughty. Didn't you know?' No. I did not!

My nicknames for Alf are Minion, because he's so small, Squishy, Pudding, Little Pea or Little Sprout, if he's being cute. They're are all much nicer than the Little Monster, even though I can't deny that he is one sometimes.

After the injection Alf was miserable for the rest of the afternoon. As soon as I walked over to him in the field he stopped eating, put his head on my leg and looked really sorry for himself, but the minute I walked away he started happily munching again. When I put him in his stable for the night he was really off with me, and when I tried to give him a kiss he put his head down so I couldn't. He had properly taken his bat and ball home.

It wasn't until I went out to see him at about ten p.m. that night he forgave me. The only reason I won him back round was because I let him eat some of the marshmallows off the top of my hot chocolate. That seems to have become a bit of routine. I'll go out to say goodnight to him and he'll nick some marshmallows. Then he's ready to go to sleep.

It is expensive having so many animals and we probably keep the vet in business but we have found ways to make things most cost-effective, such as buying all of the animals' food in bulk. Most girls my age will spend their money on clothes and make-up but my money goes on toys and treats for the animals. I love going to the pet shop and picking up things for them and I don't ever feel resentful. I would honestly rather buy things for them than for me.

Chapter 9

Galloping to Success

Somehow over the past three years I've gone from a college dropout to a fully-fledged businesswoman, or entrepreneur, or whatever you want to call me. It's crazy to write that because I didn't ever see myself in that kind of role and I didn't ever set out to have the career I do today.

I've got four companies right now: Little Alf, which obviously deals with all things Alf related, Hannah Russell Events, an events company (the name gives it away), Russell Rhino, a t-shirt based company and website dedicated to raising money to help save rhinos, and Believe It Yorkshire, an inspirational workshop business I run with my friend Dawn.

It wasn't until last year when everything was going crazy that I stopped and thought, *how did all this happen?* Am I going to have to start wearing power suits and putting my hair up in a bun?

I guess I must have always been ambitious because otherwise I wouldn't have written my first book, let alone the second, third and fourth. As I said before, I always had a passion for writing but I wasn't sure if my grammar was good enough. I looked up to so many authors and I dreamed of being like J. K. Rowling, but having a successful writing career is something that happens to other people.

The events management company started because I wanted to have a backup plan if the books stopped selling as well as they were. I wanted to have more than one string to my bow, but I'd planned to start an events company several years down the line. However, I was already going to so many events with Alfie and it struck me through that experience that the people who were probably making the real money were the ones running the shows. Sometimes there could be a hundred stands at a big event and every single one of those was being paid for – so the organisers were raking it in.

Some local events even started using Alfie to market their shows, and they were drawing really big crowds because Alf had such a big fan base. It didn't make sense. Instead of paying to go places and then making money for other people, we should be getting paid to make appearances. I was becoming much more clued up about how the events world worked and I started to plan how I could do things on my own terms.

I did three online courses: events management, international events management and wedding events management. I had a three-hour test at the end of it, and when I qualified I enjoyed it so much I set up Hannah Russell Events immediately.

I got offered work straight away, and because I was going to so many events with my books everything fitted nicely. I was organising events that I could still do signings at, and rather than paying to go, I was the one earning the money from putting the events on to start with.

The first event I put on was a fashion and gift show at Bedale Hall, in nearby Bedale. I was so nervous about how many people were going to turn up I didn't sleep the night before. Bedale Hall is massive and I really wanted to fill it. In the end it was a real success and over a thousand people came.

The events I worked on got bigger and bigger. In summer 2017 I organised a book festival with loads of Yorkshire authors, including the Yorkshire Shepherdess, as well as the Dales Food and Drink Festival, a 1940s weekend and a Christmas Fair. I've organised events for six thousand people. I've even got to the stage where I delegate work so I'm not doing it all on my own. It's odd to have people working for me, especially when they're older than me. I'm only twenty and I'm still getting to grips with how some things work and I'm learning as I go along.

Because of all these extra companies I've got eight different websites now. A lady called Katherine does all my website management for me, and she also helps me out with social media and marketing. It was a big leap for me to hand something like that over to someone else because I always like to do everything myself, but she's amazing. It feels weird that to a certain extent some of it is out of my hands but I trust Katherine's company, Reflection Media, completely. Everything goes through my business so I still check it all, but it takes some of the pressure off.

I'm the youngest member of a big events committee in Leyburn. They've been working together for years but I've been put in charge of them, which is quite daunting. Because I've done a course and I've got experience I offered to set up a spreadsheet and a programme for everyone to follow. The system worked really well, so we've stuck to it so they asked me if I'd take over and run that side of things.

I feel really bad when I need to give people instructions, but I also have to be super confident if I want to be taken seriously. At the end of the day, what does age have to do with it if you're capable? I've got a lot more experience than people twice my age who are only just starting out.

Every time I start a project my aim is to do it as best as possible. I worked with a company last year who had real issues with someone so young taking control of things so they agreed to work with me on a trial basis. The event I worked on was the first they'd ever made a decent profit on, which says it all. Since then they've left me to my own devices because they can see how on top of things I am.

I was asked to go to a meeting with another committee to have a chat about Alf potentially doing some work with them. I sat through twenty-seven points of the agenda and then when it came to talking about Alfie I gave a short talk about him and one of the women looked at his photo and said, 'What is it? That's not a horse!' Some other people laughed. At that point I wanted to get up and leave because people were being so judgemental. If I'd been a grown woman they would never have treated me that way. People have belittled me because of my age, but it doesn't concern me anymore.

It's hard to forget the people who aren't kind when you first start out, especially when they come back and ask for your help. Now my businesses are going really well those same people are inviting me to events or messaging me for advice. I do think, hang on, you weren't very nice to me. Why should I help you now? It's annoying that people didn't believe in me and they made me prove myself before they gave me any kind of respect, but all good things come to those who wait, as my nanna says!

Because I come across as 'nice' people think I'm going to be a pushover but that's definitely not the case. Never confuse kindness for weakness. You can be a good person and still be strong and capable. You don't need to be a ball-busting middle-aged man to get things done. I've always known that I don't need to throw my weight around and shout and scream because the proof of my competency is in what I do.

People do try and take the mickey out of me sometimes. They see a young girl and they think I'm gullible. I approached a clothing manufacturer for a quote on some branded Alf goods and they tried to charge a crazy amount of money for something that I knew should have been a quarter of the price. Because that company tried to stitch me up I won't ever use them again. My Alf merchandise range is growing all the time so it's their loss.

Of course I've made some business mistakes along the way but I've learnt from them. It can be hard at the time when things don't work out, but I'm really grateful for what those times have taught me. Things are going really well in all areas now but that's only because of trial and error. And there has been a lot of error.

For instance, I started a clothing range based around Alf in 2015, just before I released the second book. I didn't know anything about fashion and I invested too much into adults' clothes when it was kids who were buying my books. I was only seventeen and I didn't know a lot about business, whereas now I know to look at my target market and who comments on my blogs and pictures and I focus on them. As soon as that order arrived I knew it was a mistake and

I felt really panicky about it. I'd put a lot of money into it and the chances were I'd be stuck with a load of unsold adult-sized hoodies. The kids' stuff sold out straight away but it took ages for all the grown-up clothes to sell through.

I also started off with two Alf logos when I now know I should have just had one, as that confused people. I designed the first logo at school, before I'd even met Alf! By coincidence I designed an equestrian range as part of my GCSE textiles course, and I designed the miniature Shetland logo I still use now all that time ago. I'd even patented it. I don't know if there was some kind of sixth sense telling me I'd need it one day.

Businessmen and women and entrepreneurs have always fascinated me, even when I was younger. I loved *Dragon's Den* and I was always reading business books. It didn't hit me until I left college that it could be more than just an interest. All I knew was that I loved horses and I couldn't imagine how you could create a successful business off the back of that.

My school was more interested in the agricultural side of things so it didn't give much of a business focus. You were encouraged to stick to one path and become something practical like a farmer, a vet or a nurse. No one was ever going to say, 'Go and create your own fashion range or write a book.' So really it was up to us to work out what we wanted to do if we didn't want to follow the herd (no pun intended).

I've learnt most of what I know from books, and I've found a lot of blogs and forums very informative. When it comes to the publishing, I've learnt loads from a lady called Joanna Penn, who runs a self-publishing company called the Creative Penn. She built her company up completely on her own and she's branched out into America now. She's so helpful and encouraging to new authors.

I use a lot of other entrepreneurs as inspiration. I've never aspired to the kind of flashy lifestyle where people were boasting about their mansions and sports cars. That wasn't the kind of thing that drove me. It was more about work ethic and how they've achieved what they have. It's the people who come from very little who fascinate me. They don't come from wealthy backgrounds or have tons of qualifications, but they have ambition and they're willing to work hard and that's why they're running massive corporations.

Cathy Cassidy is a young adult author and she's written so many successful books. The best advice she gave was 'fake it 'til you make it'. I didn't get it at first and I thought it was quite a strange thing to say, but now I totally do. You've got to put your business out there and tell yourself it's doing well. You have to believe in everything you do if you want real success.

If I was going to give anyone any kind of advice about setting up their own business it would be 'don't let things get to you' and 'believe in yourself'. If you don't believe in yourself or your products it's never going to work. When I wrote my first book I didn't believe people would buy it and I didn't think it was good enough. Because of that in the early days I didn't put as much effort into promoting it as I should have done. It took me six months of telling myself every day I believed in what I was doing to convince myself I genuinely did. Now I couldn't believe in any of my businesses any more.

When I started my events management business I'd only just got my qualifications but work started coming in left, right and centre. I felt a bit nervous because it was all so new. But again, I told myself every day I was completely capable and my fear soon went away. I put on eight massive events this year alone and I feel confident about each and every one.

The more confident you are the less afraid you are to ask for what you want, and as a result you feel empowered.

People say it takes three years to establish a business and it's been three years since I first started out on this adventure. I see people quit their businesses after six months because they don't feel like trade is building as quickly as they want it to, but you've got to give it time. You've got to sit it out when things aren't going the way you want them to, and have faith that they will eventually.

As anyone who owns their own business will know, you have to be prepared to work twice as hard as you do if you're working for someone else because you're accountable for everything. I find myself working ridiculous hours and I can be up at midnight replying to emails or putting plans together, but it's so worth it. And it does balance out. If I work in the evening it means I can justify spending more time with Alf during the day.

Believe It Yorkshire is something I'm so passionate about. My partner Dawn and I put on entrepreneur workshop days where we talk about how to believe in yourself and be successful. We also have motivational speakers who come along and some of the days have been genuinely life-changing for people. We have mums who want to be able to work alongside looking after their kids. Or people who are stuck in jobs they hate. Loads go on to start up their own businesses and follow their passions, which is incredible to see.

The owner of a local farm shop came to one of our business days to get ideas on expanding his business. He's since started hosting themed nights, like games and steak nights, and their profits have gone up massively.

I did a talk to over sixty men at our local Rotary Club and afterwards they all came up to me, thanked me and said that they'd genuinely learnt a lot. One of them said to me, 'I must admit when I saw you I thought, *what on earth is this young girl going to teach me?* But you made some really interesting points and said things I've never even thought about.'

I also got asked to do a series of workshops for kids at local libraries. North Yorkshire County Council contacted me and told me that the 2017 theme for their libraries is 'Animal Agents', so the idea is to get authors who have written books about animals to talk to the children. They asked me if I'd go along and in the end I travelled to twelve different libraries and it was really lovely.

One of my favourite things I've done is when I worked on a project with a magazine called *Primary Times*, where we gave kids the opportunity to design a jumper for the Alf buddies. It was aimed at kids who were struggling to start school and didn't want to leave their mums. I remember being like that when I was a kid, and it's so sweet because we were saying to them 'don't worry if you feel sad. You can take your Alf buddy with you'. We had around five hundred entries and we had twenty of the winning jumper design made up as a limited edition buddy. It was the cutest thing.

I don't dress anything up. It's all very simple advice, but often that's the most effective. I gave a talk at a school and a young girl there told me she was desperate to write a book but she was dyslexic so didn't think she'd ever be able to. I explained my story and told her that she can do anything she wants to do. She's since written a book and got it published at her school and it's given her loads more confidence.

I often share my personal story to groups of people, and if you'd told me a few years ago I'd be up on stage in front of a big crowd chatting away I'd have thought you were mad. I used to hate public speaking. I'd mumble and say 'um' a lot because I felt so nervous, but in facing my fear I've overcome it. I feel most comfortable when I'm talking about the things I'm most passionate about and that is where it become so much easier. If you're talking about something that makes you happy it makes all the difference and it doesn't feel like an effort.

I also feel more confident if I dress well for a talk. If I'm wearing jeans and trainers I don't feel as professional, but if I wear a nice dress with tights and boots I'm good to go. I don't ever go dressed like I'm off to an office job, but making that little bit of effort puts me in a good frame of mind. I think how I'm dressed and hold myself can make a big difference. If I went to a meeting with someone about an event wearing a suit and being authoritative, no one would dare to question my abilities. But if I went in wearing a hoodie and some leggings and sat gazing around the room it would be hard to take me seriously.

There was a time when I could be easily swayed by other people's opinions but that doesn't happen anymore. I'm always really happy to listen to advice – and I do get given a lot of it – but if something doesn't sit right with me I would never just follow it because someone says I should. I doubt anyone tries to tell Peter Jones how he should run his business. Although

I always appreciate it when people are trying to help me, I don't appreciate it when they assume they know better because of how young I look.

I rely on my instinct a lot and if something feels good and is working I'll carry on. If I have any doubts I'll take a step back and re-evaluate. Even just going for a walk and spending time with my animals can help to clear my head and give me a new perspective on things.

There have been times when I haven't listened to my instincts when I should have done and things have gone wrong. When that little voice has said, 'this isn't right' I've batted it away and that's generally when things haven't gone to plan. I've also been guilty of looking to the next project rather than concentrating on the job in hand. It's easy to let things run away with you.

I feel like I'm two different people sometimes. I'll go to London for business meetings wearing smart clothes with my hair done, and then I'll come home and put on my wellies and be covered in mud within ten minutes. I think it's obvious which one I prefer. I'm sure my life would have been very different if I'd grown up in a city but you adapt to your environment. Unmade roads and endless fields are all I've ever known. When I go to a city, however exciting things are, I always feel the draw to go back home.

I think my parents were both great role models for me growing up. My dad owns an electrical design business and my mum's an artist. They're both hard workers but they balance it really well with doing all the other things they enjoy. Whatever you do in life you have to be happy. And you don't have to be earning millions to be a success. Happiness is success.

Someone said to me recently, 'Don't you think your life would be simpler if you worked for someone else?' But honestly, I don't think it would. The responsibility doesn't scare me at all. If anything, it's motivating. At the end of the day you can either build your own dream, or you can build someone else's. And I always wanted to build my own.

One of the highlights of my career so far was getting invited along to the Great British Young Entrepreneur Awards in London in November 2016. I was the only girl in my category and the first girl to be nominated in six years. At nineteen, I was also the youngest person ever to be shortlisted. I'd spent ages beforehand thinking what I was going to wear and then thankfully all my prayers were answered when ASOS sponsored me. They sent me a gorgeous full-length navy dress to wear and it was perfect for the evening. ASOS follow me on Twitter so they know when I'm going to events and they often offer to send me clothes, which obviously I'm thrilled about. Topshop also sent me some clothes from their tall range once, which was very cool. I'm so used to people sending Alfie presents so it's a nice surprise when I get some too!

The awards were held at the Lancaster Hotel in London and when we walked in everything looked so fancy. I felt a bit out of place but as soon as I started chatting to people I felt more at ease. There were thousands of people at the event but only a small amount of them were women, which I was very taken aback by. I wasn't expecting it at all. In Yorkshire it's the norm for the men to be out farming and for women to stay at home, but I thought an event like that would be much more balanced. I hope as time goes on thing even out and there are just as many businesswomen in the world as there are men.

I didn't win the main award but I came second out of six hundred entries, which felt incredible. It was the first time I'd ever been nominated for an award so that in itself felt like a massive achievement.

November 2016 was also when I launched the *Little Alf* magazine, which was another big moment. People want to know as much about Alf as they can and they're always asking me questions so it seemed like a good idea to start a mag. The idea initially came about when I was having programmes printed for my event management business. I went on the printer's website one day and saw that they also printed magazines. It was a light bulb moment. I was so excited I wrote and finished the magazine in one day, proofread it myself, and ordered copies straight away. People love the Little Alf books but they're made-up stories, whereas the magazine is a real-life glimpse into his world. My blog gets so many views I thought it would be great to adapt that into a magazine.

As well as stories the magazine has competitions, loads of photos and all the info about where people can come along and see Alf. I only ordered a hundred and fifty copies to start with because I wasn't sure how well it would sell. It sold out straight away and I had to re-order, and I started work on the follow-up issue a couple of months later.

I released my fourth book, *The Magical Adventure of Little Alf: The Hidden Secrets*, in June 2016. I left a much longer gap between the books than I had before, but I had so much going on with all my other commitments. I'd been busy creating a new Alf equestrian clothing line and that had taken up a lot of time. Alf's merchandise range was expanding constantly. I was always having new ideas for Alf goods and I really enjoyed researching the best manufacturers, costing everything up and seeing the finished product in my hands. Obviously we've got the books, clothes, magazine and teddies (which are my favourite), but now you can also get Alf tote bags, saddle pads, training bandages, bum bags – all sorts. I keep coming up with new ideas all the time.

June was quite a mixed month because the book and the equestrian range came out which was exciting, but I also broke my ankle. It was actually Alf who came to my rescue.

I was heading down the fields one afternoon to see the horses, carrying a bucket of feed in my right hand. Alf was waiting by the gate for me so I sped up a bit. Because I wasn't concentrating I stepped in a rabbit hole. I fell over one way, my foot went the other way and the bucket landed on my head and knocked me out.

I was only out for a few moments but when I

came to Alf was screaming his head off. I had this horrible searing pain in my ankle and I couldn't move to get help, but Mum came running out of the house because she'd heard Alf's distress call and knew something was up. When she saw me she said, 'Thank god it's just your ankle. I thought you'd snapped a vertebra or something.' Thankfully not, but it was still pretty painful!

There was no point calling an ambulance because it wouldn't have been able to drive across the field to get to me, so instead the farmer next door came round in his tractor, scooped me up in the front loader (the bit that's usually used to pick up dirt and logs) and took me back to the house.

My brother got me to A&E and ran off to get me a wheelchair. He kept complaining that I was heavy to push – he was trying to get me up a ramp to the entrance but he lost control of the chair and I fell into a thorn bush. Just what I needed. Because my foot was pretty much facing in the wrong direction I was rushed through to see a doctor. He took one look at me covered in scratches with thorns sticking out of my legs and asked if I'd broken my leg falling in some bushes.

I was in A&E for six hours in total and I walked

out with my foot in a massive black plastic fracture boot and facing twelve weeks of physio. During that time I had to do everything at half the speed I usually would. Mum and dad were a great help with the animals. Alf definitely knew there was something wrong because he kept licking my boot. He also bit a big chunk out of it, which the hospital wasn't too happy about.

Everyone thought it was ridiculous that I've skydived, been caving and done show jumping since I was tiny, and yet I got taken down by a rabbit hole.

I eventually got the all clear at the end of September and it was such a relief to be able to drive again. It was funny having my parents driving me everywhere again. Sometimes they'd have to take Alf and I to events and it reminded it of the early years of the book signings when we'd take Alf everywhere in my dad's van. He's got his own horsebox now so he's very posh.

After that summer Alf had a break from going to any events so he could enjoy just being a horse again. He does really like the signings and getting to meet people and show off, but we all need a break sometimes! I think given the opportunity Alf would have jetted off to the Bahamas so he could sip cocktails on a beach, but he had to settle for a rainy field in Yorkshire and extra pony nuts if he was well behaved.

Every time I thought about how much my life had changed in such a short time it made me smile. I'd gone from taking Alf to book festivals to organising them myself, and I had four books under my belt.

Things felt great. But little did I know the best was to come.

Chapter 10

By Royal Appointment

In early 2017 I received a phone call from Julia Harmby, who is the head of the Bedale and Richmond branch of the RDA, telling me that Alf and I were going to be given a special award by the RDA on 30 March. And not only that, it was going to be presented by none other than Princess Anne.

It was the twenty-fifth anniversary of the branch, and apparently since Alf and I started going it's enabled them to raise more awareness than they have done in years, which is incredibly heart-warming.

I ran straight out to tell Alf. I said, 'I don't mind

if you're naughty every day until 30 March but you must be on your best behaviour that day!' I was letting my mind run away with me, thinking about the ways he could show me up. I was visualising newspaper headlines screaming 'Princess Anne Bitten by Miniature Pony'.

What if he started biting Princess Anne's feet? Or what if she had a dress on and Alf did his party trick? And what if she was wearing strong perfume, which always makes him go a bit crazy?

As well as worrying about Alf's conduct, I was panicking about what to wear. Because Alf was coming I knew I'd have to wear trousers because he's very badly behaved if I wear a skirt or a dress. He's been known, on many occasions, to stick his head up my dress so I end up flashing people. I wore a dress when I took him to an event once and he was constantly showing passers-by my knickers.

Another time I was going for an interview with the *Yorkshire Post* and I was wearing a lovely new blue dress. The photographer was taking pictures of me and Alf outside my house and Alf pushed me over. I flashed my granny knickers at everyone and the photographer was still snapping away so he got a nice photo of it.

Mum and I spent the evening before the ceremony

messing about in the kitchen and joking about the things that could potentially go wrong, like me falling over as I tried to curtsey or Alf breaking out of his pen, making a bolt for the door and knocking over Princess Anne in the process. We were imagining all the worst-case scenarios and we were killing ourselves laughing.

The following morning I got up at five a.m. so I could bath Alfie and get him ready. There was already a big rumour going round the Dales that Princess Anne was coming to visit and it was a massive deal. I'd been thinking about what to wear since that first phone call. I was convinced I'd have one of my regular fashion meltdowns if I tried to make a decision too soon.

We got given a list of clothing requirements and they said to wrap up warm because even though we were going to be inside, it was going to be cold. It also recommended 'smart but casual attire', which I always find confusing. In the end I wore black jeans, a tweed jacket, which looks quite countrified, a floral scarf and my riding boots, which I'd polished.

It was absolutely bucketing it down with rain outside so Mum and I drove the horsebox over to Alf's stable to collect him. Helpfully, he absolutely refused to come out. After twenty minutes of trying to coax him with carrots I had to drag him to the entrance. Once he was there he hopped inside very happily because he could see it was nice and dry.

I didn't dress Alf up in anything fancy apart from a new blue head collar, which he looked very smart in. His mane and tail looked really glossy because I'd put his hair in rollers the previous night. I'd only done it so I could take some funny photos but they actually worked really well on his mane. My great-granddad Alf used to use Brylcreem and he was always telling me to use it on my horses, so as it was a special occasion I decided to give it a go. Once I took the rollers out Alf's hair was so smooth and bouncy, like he'd been to a salon. He's prone to dreadlocks but his hair had never looked better. He was spick and span and ready to roll.

We had to be properly security-checked beforehand to make sure we weren't dodgy so we arrived at the Catterick Saddle Club really early. Princess Anne wasn't arriving until two fifteen p.m. but we got there at midday to get into position. Mum, Alf and I had already been given our VIP passes, and I loved the fact they'd made a special one to go round Alf's neck.

There were fourteen blacked-out cars, armed police, five police vans and two police cars. It was pretty overwhelming. I explained to the security guards who we were and then I had to show all our passports. Yes, Alf has a passport too. It's a legal requirement for horses these days. You have to carry them at all times when you're with them. I got Alf out the horsebox and some sniffer dogs came over to check him over. You can imagine how that went down. Alf was very put out.

I think it was all a bit tongue-in-cheek but once the dogs had given him the all-clear a policeman got out a mirror on a really long handle (it looked kind of like a selfie stick) and put it underneath him to check he wasn't trying to smuggle anything in to the centre. Alf kept jumping around as if to say, 'What do you think you're doing?' Just to make finally sure he wasn't trying to get away with anything one of the policemen then patted Alfie down. Mum and I were really laughing by that point, but Alf was disgusted.

Once we were inside the ménage I had to set up Alfie's pen in our special area. Mum stood next to an old tractor with Alfie while I built it, but for some reason he took a real disliking to it. He was rearing up and trying to kick it and all sorts.

There were loads of news crews from ITV, Tyne and Tees and North East watching and they all started filming him. Then Princess Anne's bodyguards got their phones out and started taking photos of Alf bucking at the tractor.

I took Alf for a wander to calm him down but he was soon up to his old tricks and he started biting the heads off these beautiful flowerbeds that had been planted specially for the event. He spat them out and carried on walking so I had to scrape my foot over the sand and cover them over and hope no one noticed.

I put Alfie back in the van while Mum helped me carry all of his stuff in from the horsebox. I tied his hay net quite low so he could reach it and an angry woman stormed over and told me it was too low and it looked messy. I politely explained that as he's only twenty-eight inches tall, if it was any higher Alf would have needed a ladder to reach.

I finally put Alf in his pen but every time I walked off he started screaming. I had to stand next to him for two hours until Princess Anne's arrival just to keep him quiet. Because he was moulting at the time he was itching really badly. I was talking to one of the event's organisers when a volunteer came over, hit

Alf and told him to stop scratching. I was horrified. I'm so protective of Alf so I told her never to hit my pony again. She was apologetic but Alf was really upset about it. So was I.

The head of the RDA came over and apologised too but I was in shock. I wanted Alf to be himself and if he was itchy, he was itchy. At the end of the day he's a horse and they do scratch sometimes. However, I refused to let hit-gate ruin such a memorable day.

I was given a briefing about how to behave from one of Princess Anne's assistants. I had to say, 'Good afternoon, your Royal Highness,' and after that I could call her ma'am.

I was shown how to curtsey by putting one leg behind the other and bobbing my head down. It was really simple but I'm not very coordinated so I kept getting confused about which leg went behind the other. Every time I tried to curtsey I looked like I was trying to head-butt someone. It wasn't terribly dignified. I'd been trying to teach Alf to curtsey all week but there was too much happening on the day so I knew there was no way he'd do it. His attention was all over the place and the most important thing was that he behaved.

Alf and I were nervously waiting for Princess Anne

to arrive. Three of her bodyguards came over to chat to me and they started asking all about Alf. The official joined us and said to me, 'You do know you can't grab Princess Anne for a selfie, don't you?' I was giggling while I promised I wouldn't.

The bodyguards had little speakers in their hands and I heard one of them say that Princess Anne was approaching the ménage and would be inside in two minutes. I started to get a nervous feeling in my tummy. With good reason, it turned out.

Princess Anne walked in and I felt myself gasp. I thought I was nervous already but this was another level. She walked towards me and I thought, *this is crazy*. It was exciting being so close to someone from the royal family. I kept petting Alfie as if I was trying to keep him relaxed, but really it was me who needed a calming influence.

Princess Anne was due to come to us first and as she walked over I was practising my line in my head over and over again. 'It's lovely to meet you, your Royal Highness,' I said, dipping into my slightly wobbly curtsey.

'No, it's lovely to meet you and Alfie!' she replied with a smile. She told us we looked really smart and I said 'Awwwwwwww, thank you!' For some reason

I was even more Yorkshire than ever. Or maybe I just sounded that way compared to her beautifully clipped tones.

The head of the RDA explained to Princess Anne that Alf had dwarfism. Princess Anne asked me if he was supposed to be as big as a normal Shetland and when I said yes she burst out laughing, so I started laughing too.

She said, 'I'm proud to give you this award,' and then held out a lovely black and gold award. I reached out my hand to take it but before I could Alf lunged forward and grabbed it with his teeth. My head was spinning and I was thinking, please say he didn't just bite one of her fingers.

Princess Anne burst out laughing again but I was totally cringeing. I had to prise Alfie's mouth open by putting my fingers into the back of his and slowly opening it up. Eventually he dropped the award onto the ground and I managed to grab it.

I was so flustered I said, ''Ere!' and handed it back to Princess Anne covered in Alf's drool and sand from the floor. She looked down at it and said, 'Ooh, that's nice!' and someone had to hand her a tissue to wipe her hands on. Thankfully she was wearing gloves, but still . . .

She passed the award back to me and then started wagging her finger at Alf.

'No, Alfie, this is for your mummy, not for you!' she said, before calling him a cheeky monkey. She gave him a proper telling off and I loved it.

We posed for official photos and I was praying that Alf would behave, but he started pulling at the buttons on Princess Anne's coat. Thankfully she found it all hilarious and asked me loads of questions about Alf.

She was only supposed to spend three minutes with us because she was on a very tight schedule, but she was with us for over ten in the end. She asked if Alf had his own website and when I said yes she said she was going to Google him. It was so surreal.

Princess Anne had to go off and present some more awards before a riding display was due to take place. Alf was surprisingly well behaved for the first hour. Until the other horses started filing in.

Alf and I were supposed to stand quietly in the corner but I knew he'd react noisily to the other horses so I was feeding him treats to try and keep him quiet. We had all the camera crews next to us and one of the sound guys laughed and said, 'All I can hear through my headphones is your horse chomping.'

He chomps really loudly like a cow and it got so bad one of the bodyguards turned to Alf, put his finger to his lips and whispered, 'Shhhh!'

As the horses trotted nearer Alf started whinnying so the other horses got a bit agitated. He refused to be quiet so all twelve of Princess Anne's bodyguards had to stand in front of Alf's pen and block his view, which really put Alf out.

The bodyguards were wearing these square black packs on their lower backs that controlled their microphones. While I was watching the display Alf wandered over to the chief bodyguard and started pulling the wires out of his pack.

I clocked on to what he was doing so I was trying pull Alf away before the bodyguard noticed. I was saying, 'Alf, no, let go!' as quietly and firmly as I could but he wouldn't stop. He had the wires firmly between his teeth so I tried to tempt him into dropping them by offering him a Polo.

All of a sudden Alf let go of the wires, bit the bodyguard's bum and ran off to the other side of his pen. The bodyguard turned around and saw me standing there and said, 'Did you just pinch my bum?' Alf was standing four feet away, looking in totally the opposite direction and so I looked very guilty.

I looked nervously down at the microphone pack and the bodyguard followed my gaze. He saw the wires hanging out and shook his head at Alf. It turned out Alf had completely broken it and he was the person who was supposed to be passing instructions onto the rest of the security team. Someone had to run off and get him a new pack and I didn't know what to do with myself. The shame.

The embarrassment didn't end there. There was a big table next to Alf's pen with a massive cake on it. Princess Anne went over to cut the cake and it was supposed to be a really quiet, poignant moment. Alfie started to kick the bars of his pen with his hooves. He made this really loud clanging metal noise and people kept looking over. I was trying to get him to pipe down so I got into the cage with him hoping he'd stop.

He was still trying to kick the bars so I put my knee in the way. Instead of backing off he slung both of his front legs over it so it looked like he was sitting on my lap. When she saw what he was doing Princess Anne said, 'He really is a charmer, isn't he? What a personality.'

Princess Anne came back round to see us again before leaving and said, 'What a noisy little fella. He does like attention, doesn't he?'

To be honest, despite his terrible manners, I reckon Princess Anne was a bit of an Alfie fan.

After Princess Anne left loads of people came over to see Alf. There were lots of soldiers from Catterick Garrison receiving awards that day too, and they seemed more excited about meeting Alf than anyone. It was so funny seeing these burly brave men cooing over a little horse.

The cake on the table next to us was replaced with a buffet and everyone was politely waiting until they were told it was OK to tuck in. I'd told the organisers it was quite a bad idea to put the food so close to us because I knew Alf would smell it, but they assured me they'd make sure it was out of his reach.

I took my eye off him for two minutes and the next thing I knew he'd climbed up on the bars of his pen, reached over to the table and pulled the corner of a huge box of food. It all went tumbling onto the floor. He was delighted and he had his nose firmly in the middle of it all. He was eating the icing off the top of some fairy cakes and it was smothered all around his mouth. The temptation must have proved too much for him.

There were over a hundred people there that day and I don't think everyone found Alf funny, but most people were really taken with him. I'm sure some people must have thought I'm a terrible mother who needs to discipline him more, but if they tried looking after him for a few days they'd know what I was up against.

I thought maybe if I took him for a walk it might burn off some of his excess energy, but he pulled me across the ménage and I slipped on the sand and fell on my bum. The camera crews were on hand to record it all and as soon as Alf realised he was being filmed he was in his element. He was bucking and rearing and making all sorts of noises. I'm sure he just wanted all the attention back on him because everyone had been so focused on Princess Anne.

Alf and I both got individual awards that day. I got my badge, which went on display at the RDA, and Alf got his lovely black leather and gold number that fits over his collar. It says, 'long-term service and special recognition'. It looks really shiny and sleek. Until you get close up and spot Alf's teeth marks on it.

It was such an incredible day and afterwards Mum burst into tears and told me how proud of me she was of Alf and me. Dad was also overwhelmed – he said what we'd achieved was amazing. Mum, Dad and I went out for dinner that night to celebrate and Dad was even telling everyone in the restaurant about my eventful day. It was so funny because it wasn't like we knew them or anything, but Dad was literally bursting with pride and wanted everyone to know what I'd been up to.

Even though he didn't really deserve them Alf got extra treats that night. As I sat in his stable with his head on my shoulder I thought back to the first time I ever saw that funny little horse, belly deep in mud. It's just unreal how far we've come.

A few months ago I got an award for being author of the month from Lulu, the self-publishing website I publish my kids' books through, and it's so funny to think back to that first book I excitedly held in my hands and wondered if anyone would want to buy one. Now I'm plotting out ideas for future books and people seem to really enjoy them.

I recently opened a Little Alf shop in Leyburn, and it's something I'm beyond excited about. I'd had my eye on the shop for two years and when the owner phoned me to say it was available I was already designing the layout in my head. It's got a barn theme and I stock everything Alf related. He's so popular and well known in the local area, and all the tourists absolutely love him too.

I've got big plans for it and as well as selling Alf merchandise I'm going to have book signing days, workshops, magazine launches and special appearances by the miniature man himself. The scope is huge and I'm only just getting started. There's even a Little Alf trail around the Yorkshire Dales, which I've organised with Welcome to Yorkshire. Kids can start from the shop and go on a circular route around Leyburn and the Dales and see all the monuments and things to do in Yorkshire. They get a map to follow and there are clues as they go around. They also get a T-shirt saying 'I'm on the Little Alf trail'. It's so cute and it's helping to promote Yorkshire, which is something I'm really passionate about.

As well as our royal exploits, Alf and I had another funny adventure when we got invited along to the Equerry Bolesworth International Horse Show at Bolesworth Castle as part of my work with Brooke. They held a children's day where seven hundred and fifty kids came along to learn all about horses. Some of them were from inner cities, some were from underprivileged backgrounds, and some were already horse fans, so they all worked together on the day to learn more about how the horse world works.

Because Alf is a) so small and b) loves winding up other horses, he was put in the dog area because the fencing was much shorter, and he got completely spoilt. He got given a massive luxury stable to sleep in. It had his name on the door and loads of fresh sawdust. He was treated like a celebrity. We even got given a security guard to escort us round. I'm not joking.

We arrived at the event the following morning and people gathered around the horse box to see what was inside. I jokingly said it was a big dressage horse, so when I opened the door everyone peered in and started laughing. He got to parade through the main showground to his area and everyone was stroking him as we passed by.

I did six half-hour talks to the kids alongside Alf during the day. It was recorded for a channel called Horse and Country TV, and we also filmed for BBC Cheshire. They were asking me some questions about Alf and he started licking the camera so they had to stop, clean it and then start again. Then they put a big fluffy mike down next to him and he started head-butting it. I don't think they really knew what to do with him . . .

Afterwards we went into the VIP area so Alfie could have a break because he kept yawning so I could tell he was pretty worn out. There were loads of tables of free drinks and Alf started helping himself to the contents of some of the cups. I thought it was apple juice, but when I took a closer look I realized Alf was lapping up beer. I had to drag him away but he kept snorting at me and trying to pull me back over so he could have some more. We had such a fun time, but I had to make sure didn't have *too* much of a good time. I didn't want him having a hangover the following day!

Of course, I still have the odd animal drama now and again. I'd popped out to do some errands during the summer and when I came back I noticed that Paddy was standing in quite an unusual way in the corner of his field. Instinctively I knew something wasn't right so I ran down to see him.

As I got closer I noticed that there was something spurting out of him. Then I noticed the bloodstain on the fence and I panicked. I looked more closely and saw that he had a three-centimetre cut on his chest. It was like something had ripped through his skin, and it must have nicked a vein because the blood wouldn't stop coming. I hate the sight of blood but I had no choice but to try and stem the flow by putting pressure on it. My family were away on holiday so I couldn't shout to anyone for help, and I had no choice but to deal with it myself.

I dragged Paddy up to the stables and grabbed a towel from the kitchen and placed it over the wound. Then I called the vet and they gave me some instructions over the phone so I could try and stop the bleeding. They wanted me to go and get some bandages, but because no one else was in I couldn't leave him or ask anyone else to go and get them for me.

The bleeding seemed to be getting worse instead of better and I was so worried. In the end, a vet had to come out and put some stitches in it, and it was only once it was sealed the bleeding stopped.

The vet left and I thought that was that, but within an hour the stitches burst and the wound began bleeding again. I took another cloth and applied more pressure and sat with Paddy for ages. The bleeding kept stopping and starting. Every time there was a small break I was able to go and see to the other animals and make sure they were fed and watered, but I couldn't leave Paddy for very long.

I first noticed the injury at three p.m., but it took until nine p.m. for it to stop bleeding completely.

Thank goodness Paddy was calm because I really wasn't. I thought he'd been really distressed but instead all he wanted to do was eat. I think he was probably comfort eating to take his mind off what was going on.

Thankfully he seemed a lot better the following morning, but even now there's a lump there and he doesn't like anyone touching him in that area. I've got no idea how the injury happened. At first I thought it was a nail hole, but when my dad got back from holiday we searched all the fences to see if anything was sticking out and we didn't find anything. It's a total mystery, but I'm so glad I was there to help him.

It doesn't even bear thinking about that Alfie shouldn't really be here. Most breeders would have destroyed him early on. Writing that sentence fills me with horror. Even though he's fit and well, because of his dwarfism he's prone to illness so I am more cautious with him than I am with my other horses. Lots of mini Shetlands born with dwarfism are in a lot of pain and can have a short life expectancy, which is obviously something I'm very conscious of.

The normal life expectancy for a horse is twenty to

forty years. Badger is my oldest at twenty-eight and he's as a fit as fiddle, touch wood. He should live up until his mid to late thirties.

Our vet reckons Alf's pretty sturdy and Shetlands are known for being strong so I'm hopeful he'll live to a good age. I know a Shetland at my local stables who is forty-two. I also read about a Shetland with dwarfism in America who lived until the ripe old age of fifty, so you just never know.

As long as Alf keeps physically healthy he should be fine, and because I've looked after him from such a young age he's always had the best care and attention.

There's such a lot of snobbery about dwarf ponies and people need to start being more accepting. It's not the horse's fault they're born the way they are, and they have just as much right to a happy life as any other animal.

It amazes me that people are still so elitist in this day and age. I tried to register Little Alf with the Shetland Pony Society but they refused to let him in. The lady who phoned me to tell me the news felt terrible about it, but she said they couldn't accept him. I also wanted to put an advert for my books in their magazine. Again, they refused, even though a percentage of the book profits were going to the

RDA. They said they didn't want to encourage people to breed horses with dwarfism, but that wasn't what it was about. I would never encourage people to breed horses with problems. But why not look after the ones that are born?

Alf has become more and more affectionate as time has gone on. He's also more needy – he's a big baby really. He seems really settled and happy and I think he loves living with us. Because of that I would say Alf is exactly where he should be. I can't imagine him being as happy anywhere else. I had to rub Sudocrem on his bum the other day because he had some chafing. Then I let him have a wander around our kitchen and fed him some posh carrots from the fridge to cheer him up. If he's left out for too long he gets very cold and stiff and I've sat in his stable in the freezing cold giving him massages before. I'm not sure everyone would be prepared to look after him the way my family and I do.

I always say to Mum and Dad that I have no idea what I'd be doing career-wise now if Alf hadn't come along when he did. My life would be completely different.

I don't want to blow my own trumpet and say that I saved Alf but I think maybe I did. I like to think so. But by the same token, he saved me. He brings so much joy to me and all the people he meets. Apart from when he passes wind or tries to nick people's sweets, obviously.

There are times when I still miss riding and I have days when I long to get on a horse and gallop off into the woods. But all I have to do is look at Alf and everything feels great again.

Sometimes people laugh when I refer to myself as Alf's mum, but that's how I see it, and I know that's how he sees it. I am his mum and he's the best thing that's ever happened to me.

My life wouldn't be complete without him.

Epilogue:
Christmas with Little Alf

I'd like to round off the book by telling you just how special my Christmases with Little Alf are. It will always be such an important time for me because it was when I he came to live with me, and since his arrival the festive season has been more magical than ever.

I definitely see Alf as my child and I start planning and buying him presents for Christmas as early as October. I get things when I see them and I store them up ready, as I do with all the other horses. I usually but them toys and food treats, both of which they absolutely love.

All the horses' stables get decorated with tinsel, and they all have some kind of sign on the door. Alfie has one saying 'Santa, please stop here!' (so that Father Christmas knows where to deliver his presents, obviously).

Alf loves snow globes so last year I bought him one with a polar bear inside that sits on a ledge in his stable. When I shake it he'll stare at it and watch as all the snow falls down. He's also a fan of fibre optic trees. He's mesmerized by them when they're twinkling and changing colour.

He adores the baubles on our Christmas tree, but we have to watch him at all times because he's got a habit of breaking them. I decorated the tree with him last year and he kept brushing himself up against the branches and licking the baubles. He ended up ruining two very old decorations that had belonged to my great-nana, so my mum wasn't very impressed.

On Christmas morning I go straight to see Alf as soon as I wake up, and I take his presents with me. I wrap them up really nicely with ribbon and I put them in his sack, which has his name on it. Of course he always needs a bit of a hand opening them so he'll nudge them and look at me as if to say 'why aren't you helping me?'

If I'm being honest I don't think Alf's too fussed about my careful wrapping. He just wants to see inside and get his teeth on things as quickly as he can (especially food). He gets sent a lot of presents from fans these days, and my family always buy him little things too. The most unusual present he got last year was a tambourine, but I haven't managed to teach him to pick it up and play it yet. He definitely gets more presents than me but that's the way I like it.

I like to put reindeer ears on Alfie on Christmas morning, and he gets a special breakfast, which is a mix of pony nuts, a few Polos and some olive oil, which makes his coat nice and shiny.

He gets to have a lie in, which he loves, while I go back into the house and open my own presents with my family, and then he gets to come in and hang out with us on Christmas afternoon. One year we even let him watch the Queen's speech with us.

Alf likes to eat all day and as well as munching on carrots and apples he, Badger, Paddy and Pepper will share the peelings from the Christmas dinner vegetables. Alf loves a turnip as a treat but they make him very gassy so they're kept to a minimum. If he does get one on Christmas day he'll have to wait until he's safely back in his stable to eat it so we don't suffer the consequences.

I always go and say goodnight to Alf right before I go to bed, and sometimes I'll tell him a little Christmas story to send him to sleep. People might think he doesn't understand them but I'm sure he does. I like to believe he does anyway!

Acknowledgements

There are so many people I need to thank but firstly I can't believe I'm actually writing some Acknowledgements! If you'd told me three years ago that Little Alf would one day have his memoir published I wouldn't have believed it, which leads me to think that dreams can come true with hard work, determination and a lot of coffee . . .

First and foremost I need to thank my Mum, Dad and brother John for supporting me from day one. Especially my mum for reassuring me on the days I have meltdowns, and for believing in me as a person.

You've really kept me going over the past few years and without you I wouldn't be where I am today.

A special thank you also to my Dad, who has taught me you have to do whatever makes you happy in life, and for chauffeuring me and Alfie around the UK to book events – even when the weather has been cold and wet. You've both played a huge role in where I am today and couldn't feel more lucky to have parents like you both.

A huge thank you to Jordan for working with me on this book. It's been an emotional rollercoaster, we've had lots of laughs and it's been fantastic to work with you. I couldn't think of a better, kinder person to work with, you truly are amazing. A special shout out to Doreen and Jeremy – you're the most adorable dachshunds I've ever seen.

A special thank you to my amazing editor Rhiannon (I think you now share the same love of Alf as I do!) and everyone at Little, Brown Book Group for sharing my story with the world and making it into a book, I truly feel blessed to be working with such a great company.

This book would not have happened without my agent Philippa and, of course, Elizabeth, your enthusiasm for the book at the very beginning has kept me excited from the day we began working together. I must admit at the time the idea for the book sounded pretty random and crazy but you believed in us from the very start! You've been such a joy to work with over the past year and it's been quite a journey seeing how the publishing world works – it's been the most exciting experience.

A thank you to my partner Jonny for being behind me every step of the way and putting up with me when I've wanted to spend more time with Alfie than you . . .

To all my pets, past or present, you've all played roles in the person I am today and this book. My life is so full of furry friends and I could not imagine it any other way.

Thank you to everyone who picks up this book and reads our story, to those who have supported me over the past few years on my Alf journey, to anyone who's watched our YouTube Videos, read the Little Alf books or visited us at a book event, although I can't name you all individually I really appreciate every single one of you, it really means a lot.

Lastly I have to thank my little pea who you all know as Little Alf, from the moment I met you you've always put a smile on my face and I truly couldn't imagine my life without you. You're my partner in crime and you've changed my life forever. Everyone needs an Alf in their life to brighten up their day.

Follow Little Alf

You can find out more about Little Alf via his online
website: www.littlealf.com
Or head over to his social media channels to keep up
with all his latest adventures:
Twitter: @AlfLittle
Facebook: @HannahRussellAuthor
Instagram: @Little_Alf_

Little Alf shop

Visit the Little Alf shop in Leyburn Market Town, North
Yorkshire. In 2017 Hannah & Little Alf opened their first shop
together, located in the heart of the Yorkshire Dales and full of
Little Alf pictures and products! You can visit the shop 4 days
a week, and you can now also experience the 'Little Alf Trail
Around the Yorkshire Dales' from the shop which will take you
on a tour of the local area.

Shop Address (located behind the golden lion)
Little Alf
1 Golden Lions Yard
Leyburn,
North Yorkshire
DL8 5AS